CREATED BY GOD

Tweens, Faith, and Human Sexuality

Written by James H. Ritchie, Jr., Ed.D.

Nan Zoller, Editor/Contributor

Created by God
Tweens, Faith, and Human Sexuality

ISBN 978-1-426-70040-8

Dr. James H. Ritchie, Jr., Writer
Nan Zoller, Editor/Contributor
Marcia Stoner, Supervising Editor
Marjorie M. Pon, Editor, Church School Publications
Karen Scholle, Production Editor
Keitha Vincent, Designer

Art Credits:
Cover Design Concept: Ken M. Strickland
Pages 27, 50, 56: Brenda Gilliam
Pages 5, 13, 14, 23, 42, 45: Mike Meredith
Pages 18, 42, 70, 96: Robbie Short
Pages 27, 28, 32, 34, 35, 48, 57, 66, 67, 68, 89, 91, 94: Sarah Smith
Page 12: Randy Wollenmann
Page 63: Big Cheese Photos
Pages 4, 8, 65, 86, 95, 114: Liquid Library
Page 9: United Methodist Communications

09 10 11 12 13 14 15 16 17 18—10 9 8 7 6 5 4 3 2 1
MANUFACTURED IN THE UNITED STATES OF AMERICA

PACP00457026-01

Written by James H. Ritchie, Jr., Ed.D.

Nan Zoller, Editor/Contributor

Contents

Introduction 

Why Do I Have to Go Through All This?

Why do I have to go through all of this?

Why are my parents giving me books about sexuality?

Why did they sign me up for this study?

Why do I need information about my body, growing up, relationships, reproduction, responsibilities, and how faith in God makes a difference?

Why will my body go through all these changes?

Ready or not, like it or not, you are heading into **adolescence** (*A-doh-LES-sens*) — the time of growing and changing from a child to an adult. With that growing comes changes in your body, mind, spirit, emotions, and responsibilities. Those changes will be physical, emotional, spiritual, mental, and relational. That's a lot! And your parents and your church want to help you navigate those changes.

> *What does God and the church have to do with it?*

You were created by God! And God is still at work in you, moving you along the path designed for you from your creation, through childhood, and now towards adulthood. Yes, you've been moving along that path since you were born, but now it's time for you to pick up speed! In these next few years you'll be making major changes toward becoming an adult: how you look, how you feel, how you think, and how you relate with other persons.

So how does "sex" come in? God made us male or female, to live and love, to form relationships and families, and gave us the privilege of creating new human life. God gave us the gift of our sexuality—our maleness or femaleness—and like all of God's creation, said "It is good."

Working from a mental image or picture,
God created humankind;
Out of the Creator's imagination they were created;
Male and female God created them ...
God surveyed all God had made,
And declared all of it to be outstanding.
Evening and morning marked the sixth day of creation.

(Genesis 1:27 and 31,
paraphrased)

While some people may try to tell you that sexuality is something evil or apart from God, we want you to know that your sexuality, your body, and your expressions of physical love are all gifts from God for you to understand and to use very wisely.

The information you will find in this book is intended to help you be proud and confident about being female or male. And to give you right information that will protect you from the many kinds of wrong information and dangerous attitudes you will likely hear and encounter. With a positive attitude toward God's good gift of your sexuality, you'll be able to make good decisions and to be a healthy example of a Christian to others.

So, let's find out more!

9

Chapter 1

Changes Happening

Have you ever wondered what it was like for Jesus as a tween? Do you think he ever spent time daydreaming? What do you think he looked forward to when he was "all grown up"? What were the signals that helped him know he was maturing as a human being and as God's child?

We find insights about Jesus' childhood only in the Gospel of Luke, chapter 2, verses 41-52. Here we see the story of Jesus, with his family, traveling to Jerusalem for the Passover festival. Each spring they would worship in the Temple there, joining friends and family in a meal that used special words, foods, and actions to remember how—many centuries earlier—God had delivered the people of Israel from Egyptian slavery.

But this year was different, one that had been anticipated by Jesus and his parents since he was born, twelve years before. According to Jewish tradition, young males at twelve were received into "adulthood" in the eyes of the worshiping community through a ceremony called a bar mitzvah (MITS-veh), which means "son of command" or "son of godly living." As such, Jesus would have new privileges such as worshiping with the men and new responsibilities for helping to keep the faith alive. He would also be expected to make wise choices. In many ways, this visit to Jerusalem and to the Temple would celebrate his growing up.

No minivans with roof racks piled high and traveling in caravan for the families from Nazareth! More likely, the Jewish families going to Jerusalem from the tiny town about 65 miles to the north, walked with perhaps a donkey or two to carry a few possessions. And chances are they didn't walk in individual family groups. You can probably visualize the men walking and talking together, the women with the youngest children, and the older children running along between the two groups, playing games and shouting as they go. And no motels along the way! Travel to Jerusalem involved several nights of camping as they walked through the valleys and over the hills and mountains.

13

Finally, they arrive! Jerusalem is bustling with thousands of Passover pilgrims. Every day Jesus visits the Temple, listening eagerly as the teachers read and explain the meaning of Torah (God's Word or law for the people). He sees the sacrifices offered to God and participates in the bar mitzvah ceremony granting him the privileges and responsibilities of a Jewish adult.

But then the week is over, and the pilgrims begin leaving for their remote villages. Mary and Joseph gather their belongings, join the Nazareth group, and begin the long walk. Mary may wonder why Jesus isn't there to help pack up, but then likely thinks that since the bar mitzvah, Jesus is with his father and the other men. Maybe she smiles at the thought of her special son. And Joseph, with the other men, likely assumes that Jesus is traveling with his mother, just as he has always done. He may realize that despite the ceremony, Jesus is still a child in many ways and may be with the other children.

Evening comes, and at the campsite Mary and Joseph realize that Jesus is not with either of them. They check throughout the entire caravan and realize with panic that their son is not with the group. Of course, they start the day's journey back to Jerusalem at the first light. Imagine your parents' reaction if this had happened to them!

For another three days they search the city. Jesus has now been missing as many as five days. The last remaining place to look is the Temple. Stunned, Mary and Joseph find him sitting at the feet of the teachers, listening carefully to all they had to say. So much to absorb!

How would he ever take it in? Faces full of amazement, the
teachers listen to the questions and answers Jesus offers. And what relief
for Mary and Joseph! Then those feelings may have turned to
bewilderment and even a bit of anger. Why would Jesus do such a
thing? Jesus must have seen the worry and fear, because he asks,
"Didn't you know that I had to be in my Father's house?" sounding
surprised that his parents didn't know where he would be.

The story ends with these words: "And Jesus increased in wisdom
and in years" (getting wise and older), "and in divine and human favor"
(growing in his relationships with God and with others) (Luke 2:52).

As Jesus traveled with his family to Jerusalem and back, he was
also in the midst of his journey of **adolescence** (a-doh-LES-sens), the
period of growth between childhood and adulthood. Like you, he was
growing, wondering, testing, and discovering what it meant to be an
adult. His body was changing in many ways—with new feelings and
sensations. New muscles and new coordination were likely evident.
Surely his interests began to change from those of a child. And while his
family remained very important to him, he was also developing
relationships outside his family. All this was very normal then, and it's
normal for you now.

🚻 Constant Change

You may be twelve, or maybe you are nine, ten, eleven, or thirteen
as you read this book. Think about how you have grown and changed
in the past few years—in obvious ways that have caused others to
comment and in minor ways that only you have noticed. Have you
wondered, *Am I supposed to be growing this fast? Should I be growing
faster? How long is this going to continue? Why can't I look like
everyone else? Do other kids feel as awkward as I do? Am I weird? Is
this normal?*

Normal is change. And normal change is specific to YOU. What
we mean is that there is no exact timetable for change that all
adolescents follow. As a pre-adolescent or an adolescent, you will be
experiencing dramatic growth and change over the next several years—
the noticeable and the unnoticeable. All that is perfectly normal,
predictable, and even desirable. And it will be on your own timetable.

Stop and think: have you noticed changes in your energy level—one moment you're ready to run a marathon with energy to spare, and the next you're so tired you could fall asleep on your feet? What about sudden shifts in your emotions—you're laughing happily with your best friends when, without warning, you find yourself angry at them as though they were your worst enemies? Do you seem to have suddenly outgrown your clothes? And do you ask yourself, *What are these changes in my body?*

> NOTE: The **words** you see **printed in this kind of type** are ones you can find in the glossary located in the back of the book. The words you might have difficulty pronouncing are accompanied by a pronunciation guide. Accent the capitalized syllable.

Name That Change

Think back two years. What kind of changes have you noticed in yourself? Below are some categories to help you identify some changes.

- My Changing Mind:
  Things I think about or know now that I didn't think or know about.

- My Changing Emotions:
  New or stronger emotions and ones I no longer have or that aren't as strong.

- My Changing Faith:
  Differences in how I understand and connect with God and what I do about those understandings and differences.

- My Changing Relationships:
  Friends I've made, friends I've lost, and other changing relationships, including within my family.

Remember the verse Luke 2:52 about Jesus increasing in wisdom? That reminds us that he didn't know everything from the beginning. He had to grow up just as you are doing. As his body matured, so did his mind. He was discovering that life is much more complicated than how he saw it as a child. He was growing in his ability to make choices based on what he knew and how his decisions would affect others. As he grew he was learning to live responsibly:

> **Responsible**
> **Response-able**
> **Able to respond with maturity**
> **Able to respond faithfully**
> **Response-able**
> **Responsible**

You're learning to live responsibly too, becoming more aware that what you do affects many persons, not just yourself. To do that, you need information and understanding in order to grow in wisdom as Jesus did. You must set goals for yourself and plan for your life. And you must carefully choose your mentors and life-teachers. You're recognizing that life is complicated, asking questions is crucial, and putting God at the center of your life is essential.

In all this, you will want to be more independent, to make your own decisions, and to take greater control of your life. And for that you need wisdom in all areas, especially about your self and your body.

Families aren't addresses, houses, or names. Families are people. Sometimes families live in the same house, and sometimes they don't. Sometimes family members all have the same name, and sometimes they don't. Some members are born into the family while others are adopted in, married in, or just loved into the family for a variety of reasons. Some families have lots of children, and some have none. There are families with two parents, some with one, some with grandparents or some other family members, or foster parent.

So, what makes a family a family? More than marriage licenses, birth certificates, or adoption papers, a shared and caring life together defines a family. Families share experiences and connections, they care for and are committed to one another. And family members are interconnected: one person's changes impact the entire family, and your changes throughout adolescence will impact your family.

Who's in your family? Stop for a second, and around the oval "table" on the top of page 19, place your family. Draw a symbol for yourself and one for each member of your family, whether or not they live in the same house.

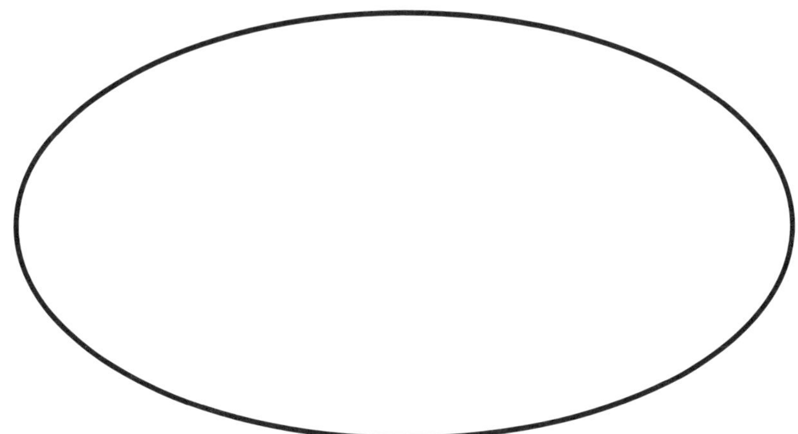

Once you have assembled your family (mentally or actually), draw lines between your symbol and each family member's symbol, representing the connection you feel with each person. Consider what this says about your family and about changes that are happening.

Don't worry: many changes are good ones! Your parents will begin to trust you to do things you weren't allowed to do when you were younger (going to the movies without a parent or baby-sitting for younger children), and you'll be allowed to take on new responsibilities (like driving or getting a job). On the other hand, change also means new limitations. Actions that were acceptable from you as a child are no longer appropriate (failure to keep your room tidy or throwing temper tantrums). As you move toward adulthood, you can say with the apostle Paul, "When I was a child, I spoke like a child, I thought like a child, I reasoned like a child; when I became an adult, I put an end to childish ways" (1 Corinthians 13:11). Families help us discover what is and isn't appropriate behavior, although it isn't always an easy process for anyone! As you and your family grow and change together, you will be making such discoveries.

Communication is the key to positive change and growth. The healthiest adolescents are those who are able to communicate with adults who care about them, especially their parents. And, those same adolescents are least likely to engage in potentially destructive behaviors (like drug and alcohol use, sexual experimentation, and taking unnecessary physical risks), and most likely to demonstrate respect for themselves and others.

When I became an adult, I put an end to childish ways. (1 Corinthians 13:11)

All of us were created in the image of God. Like God, you have a hand in the creation of something new—the new person you are becoming. You are God's work-in-progress. God is at work in you, shaping a mature body, mature mind, mature feelings and relationships, and a mature faith. Those who love you are watching with great anticipation to see the new you emerge.

Remember: "And Jesus increased in wisdom and in years, and in divine and human favor" (Luke 2:52). What happened to the young Jesus over 2000 years ago is now happening to you.

Welcome to adolescence! You are growing and changing, becoming the adult God plans for you to be!

Chapter 2

Fantastic Female and Marvelous Male

She bodies, he bodies, each one unique;
every conceivable size and physique.
Yours is the special one God had in mind.
Look in the mirror and there you will find—

O what a wonderful, marvelous, glorious,
what a fantastic creation we are!
When I look all around I am reminded
we're far more amazing than earth, sea, and star! *

"Oh, I already know all that stuff!" said Brenda to a friend when she heard that her church was planning a study on human sexuality. "Me, too!" said the friend. "I already told my parents I'm not going."

Maybe you've said the same thing. After all, you and your friends talk some (and maybe giggle or make jokes) about sex. You may discuss it every once in a while with a parent or another adult. Perhaps you have an older brother or sister who answers your questions from time to time. It could be that you've read a book or looked at pictures. Maybe you've had a class in school that described how girls grow and develop if you're a girl or how boys grow and develop if you're a boy.

22

* "What a Fantastic Creation We Are," words and music by James Ritchie.
© 1984, 1987, 1999, 2009 by James Ritchie. Used by permission.

So, let's agree that you already know some important stuff about how your body functions. However, most girls are curious and could use some additional information about boys. Likewise, most boys are curious and could use some additional information about girls. Why? Because we live in a world where people come in two genders. Wouldn't it seem odd for us not to understand half of the human race? So, here's a chance to see the whole picture!

The Bible starts with these words: "In the beginning when God created the heavens and the earth," or "When God began to create the heavens and the earth …" The thoughts and understandings of ancient people were tied to the earth. They had no sense of a vast universe and earth's very small part. It makes sense that they would speak of creation beginning with the earth at the center, set in the great unknown that they called the heavens.

The only sign of life in this great, deep, damp, dark, swirling sameness was the breath of God. God, who has always been, was present in the beginning. And with the word, "Light!" God begins creating. With the creation of light, what had been uncertain and formless takes shape. Isn't that what happens when you turn on the light in a dark room?

Night and day; waters above (clouds and rain) and water below (rivers and oceans); dry land covered with vegetation in the midst of the seas. All of the sameness is disappearing. With time for waking and sleeping in place and food growing on the land, the scene is set for animals—fish swarming in the seas and birds flying through the air. With each addition of differences, God speaks another word: "Good!"

Next come the animals on the land, and the ones called "humans" —Adam and Eve—were specifically created in the image of God. We are part of God's creation and a valuable part of God's plan. What does it mean to be made like God? It means that we have within us the ability to create—to create beauty, to create peace, to create loving relationships, and even to create new life with God. For the creation of new life, God made us male and female. This kind of creating calls for the cooperation of people who are different from each other in many important ways. For the creation of new life, God made us male and female. The fact that God created two different genders (male and female) of many animals, including human beings, reminds us of the interdependence of humankind. We need each other in order for our kind to survive, in order to become all that God has planned for us.

24

There's no time in our lives that we aren't changing! From birth to our last breath, our bodies are changing. But there are certain times when we change more quickly and dramatically than at other times. Infants and toddlers grow and change almost from month to month. Another time of rapid and significant change is the one you are entering now, called **puberty** (PEW-bur-tee), which is when the body changes from that of a child to that of an adult, and when the sex organs mature, beginning to produce mature ova or sperm. Let's think specifically about the internal and external changes taking place in your body right now—some of them seen, but most of them unseen, preparing you to realize fully the joy that God has planned for people to experience with their bodies.

All changes are easier to deal with when we have some idea of what to expect and are able to talk about them. Especially these changes. In order to communicate clearly, we need to make sure we have a common vocabulary related to the parts of our bodies that make us male and female, and how these body parts function. So, let's begin our tour of female and male bodies.

Everybody's Got Them

First let's be sure we know about the body parts we have in common. The area between our legs is known as our **genitalia** (JEN-uh-TAIL-yuh) or **genitals** (JEN-uh-tuhls), and is defined as the external (outside) male and female sex organs. (Maybe your family has called this your "private parts.") **Pubic** (PEW-bick) hair begins growing in the genital area and below the **abdomen** (AB-doh-muhn), or belly, beginning at the start of puberty. We all have two openings for bodily waste. The **anus** (AY-nuhs), the opening where solid waste leaves the body, is neither part of the vulva nor of the reproductive system, but we refer to it because it is located in the same general area, just a few inches below the vulva. The other is the **urethra** (yoo-REE-thruh), which is the narrow tube through which urine passes out of the body from the bladder. In males the urethra is a part of the reproductive system and is a passageway for semen and sperm. Lastly, let's not forget the **breasts.** Breasts you say? Yes, breasts are the two glands on the upper chest of both males and females, and their growth is stimulated at puberty. In females the breasts develop more fully so that they can produce milk following the birth of a child.

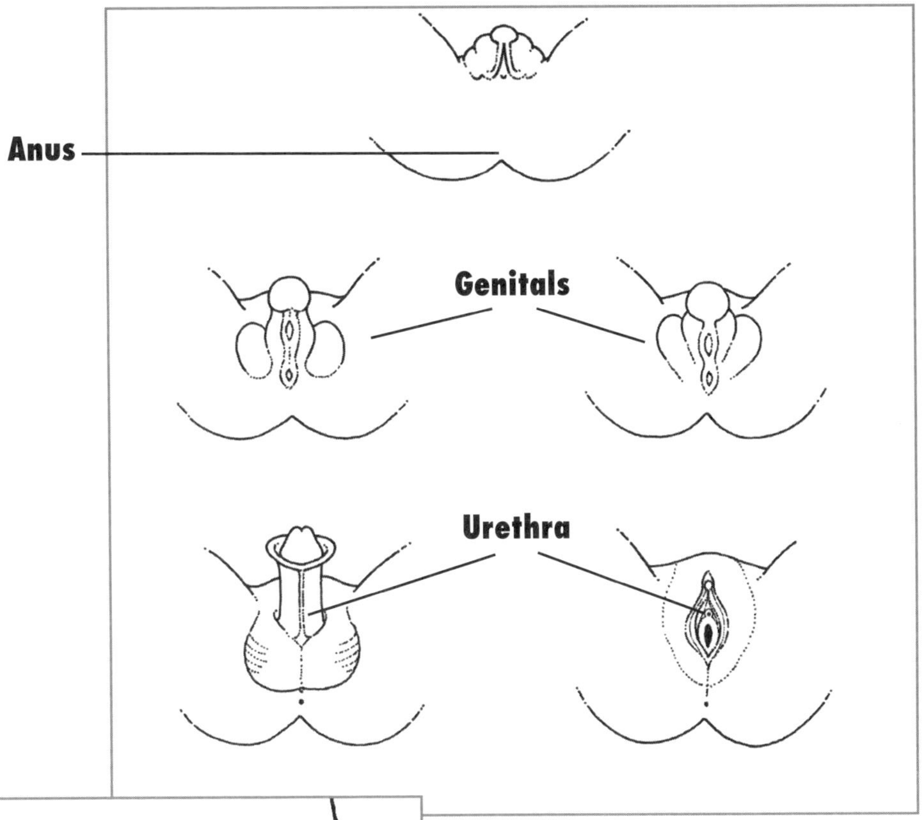

Anus
Genitals
Urethra
Abdomen 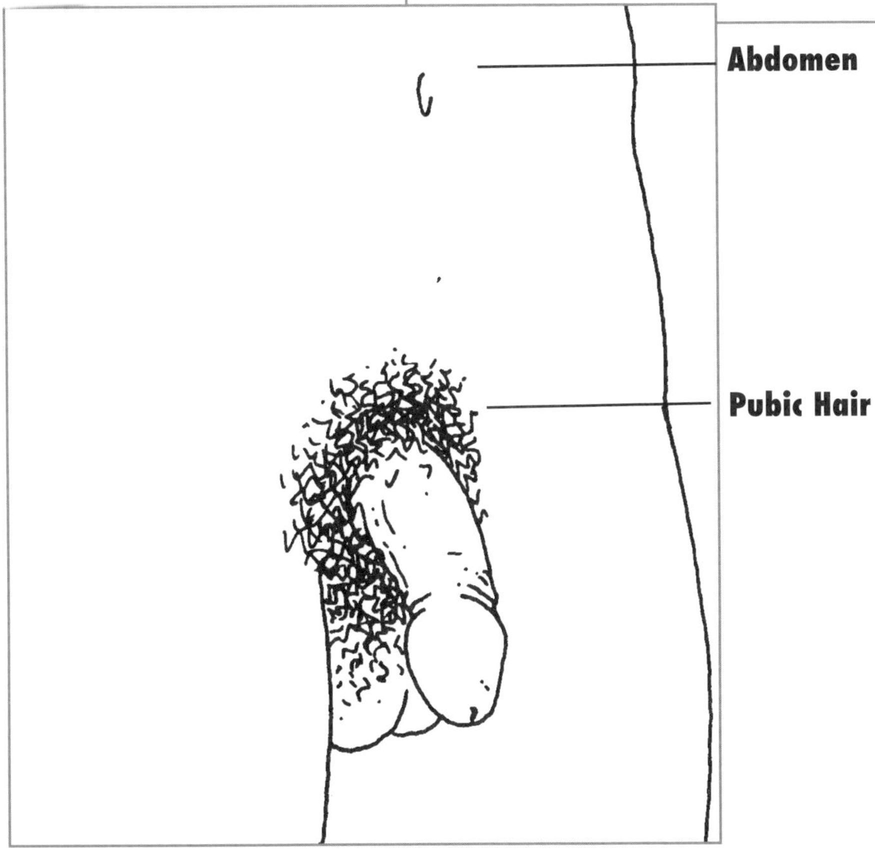
Pubic Hair
27

Male Reproductive System (external view)

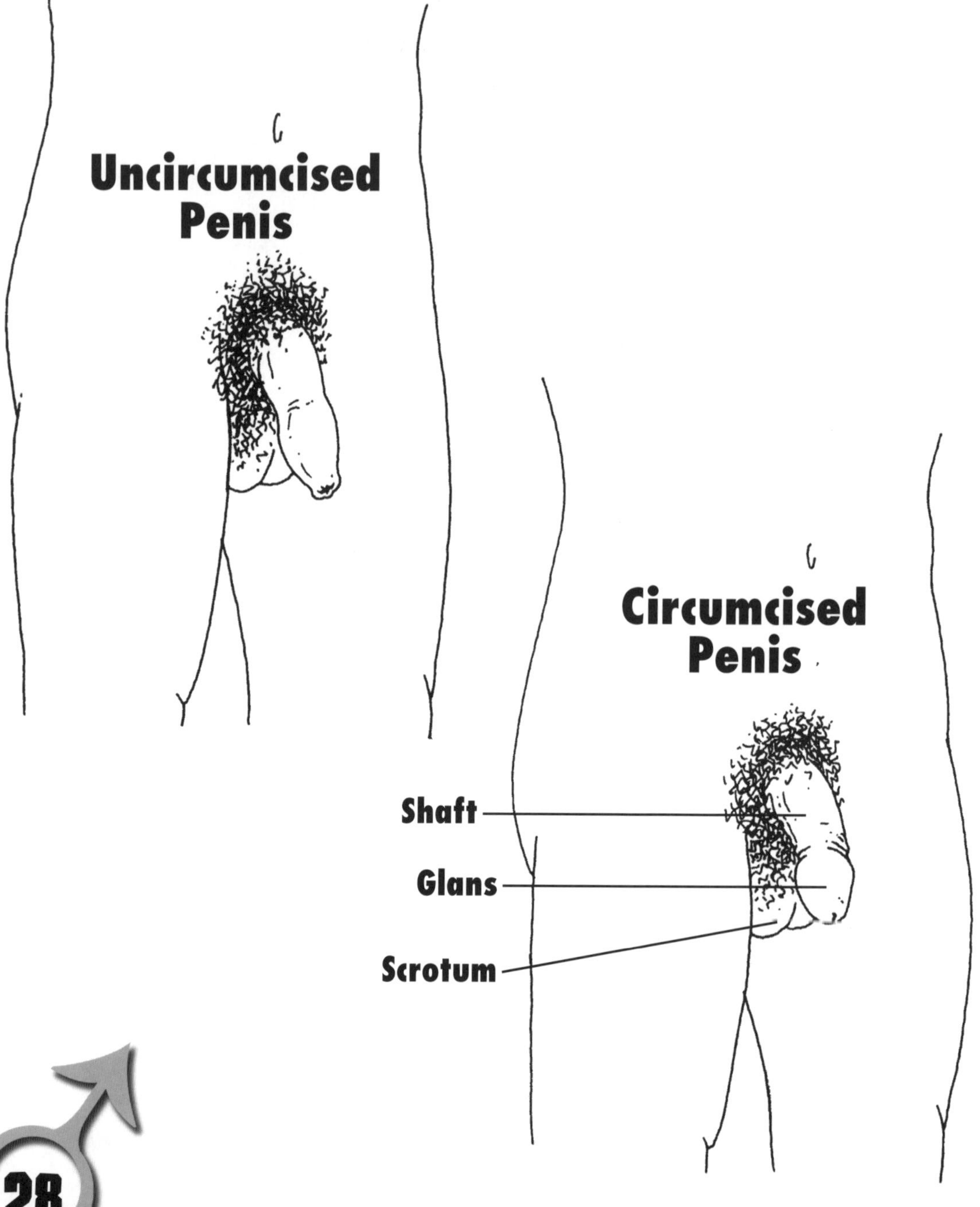

We start with the male body because boys have bodily parts that are visible. And the first defining difference between boys and girls is that a boy has a **penis** (PEE-nuhs). It is the cylinder-shaped part of the male genitals. Slang terms abound, but penis is the term we need to practice using. The cylinder part of the penis is called the **shaft.** The end or head of the penis is called the **glans.** The penis (especially the glans) is the most sensitive part of the male genitals. The opening to the urethra in males is at the end of the glans. Remember that the urethra is the passageway for urine to exit the body and in males is also part of the reproductive system.

Another part of the penis is the **foreskin** (FOR-skin). The shaft of the penis is covered with a loose layer of skin, and when boys are born, that skin extends down over and covers the glans. It is open at the end so urine can be released. An operation called **circumcision** (sir-cum-SIZH-un) in which a doctor removes the foreskin is often performed shortly after birth. This operation is sometimes done for religious reasons (see page 30), sometimes for cultural reasons (some cultures, countries, or regions of a country do not practice circumcision while others do), sometimes for hygienic reasons (to prevent infection), and sometimes for family reasons (so sons look like their circumcised dad).

Though circumcised and uncircumcised penises look different, they all feel and function the same. Occasionally, a boy or man who was not circumcised in infancy may decide, with his doctor, that circumcision is necessary later on in life.

Curious kids have often asked, "Why would people decide to cut off a part of a boy's body? In the United States, a majority of boys are circumcised as babies, but not all. In other parts of the world it is just the reverse, with more boys remaining uncircumcised. For some people, circumcision is a religious custom. You may first have heard or read the word *circumcision* in the Bible, and that is where we need to go to understand this practice.

In the days of Abraham, God was establishing a distinctive people who would later become known as the Hebrews or Israelites. With these people and starting with Abraham, God made a covenant to be their God, and the people in turn responded with faith, loyalty, and a "mark" of that covenant. That mark was and is today circumcision for the Jewish people.

Another factor was that water for washing was not always available, making it far more difficult to keep clean than it is today. For uncircumcised men, the failure to wash under the foreskin could lead to the collection of bacteria and an infection, which could prevent a man from having sexual intercourse and fathering children. Parents were believed to be blessed by God when they had children. Is it any wonder that circumcision became a religious tradition for the descendants of Abraham—both Jews and Muslims?

Inside the Marvelous Male

Beneath the penis is the **scrotum** (SKRO-tum), the pouch or sack of skin which hangs from the body. Inside the scrotum are the two **testicles** (TESS-tih-kuhls), egg-shaped organs that produce chemicals called **hormones** (HOR-mohns) and the male reproductive cells called **sperm**. Sperm are microscopic in size, but under strong microscopes we can see that they are shaped like tiny tadpoles with a tail-like piece that helps propel them. (We'll discuss hormones more in Chapter 3.) Guys will notice that one of their testicles (generally the left) hangs lower than the other. This is God's design to prevent these very sensitive organs from getting knocked together during physical activity.

In order for sperm to be produced, the testicles must be a few degrees cooler than normal body temperature. Each testicle is suspended (hangs) in the scrotum by the small **cremaster muscle** (krih-MASS-ter) that acts as a thermostat, drawing the scrotum and testicles up closer to the body when they are cold, and lowering them when they are warm. Also, when a male is frightened or threatened, his testicles will draw up closer to the body, protecting them from injury.

The testicles are made up of about 250 little compartments, and each compartment contains tiny thread-like tubes. Attached to the back of each testicle is an **epididymis** (ep-uh-DID-uh-mis), another mass of tiny tubes. The sperm produced in the testicles mature during the four to six weeks it takes for them to travel through the epididymis to the **vas deferens** (VAZ DEHF-uhr-uhnz), which is a 14- to 18-inch long tube that loops up over the bladder and then gets gradually larger in diameter. The sperm that have been produced in the testicles and mature in the epididymis are moved through the vas deferens to it's end, called the **ampulla** (am-POOL-uh), where they are stored. Nearby are the **seminal vesicles** (SEM-uh-nuhl VESS-ih-kuhls) which make a whitish fluid called **semen** (SEE-muhn) that is critical to the reproductive process. Semen looks a lot like the white part of a raw egg.

The **prostate gland** (PROSS-tate) is located beneath the bladder, at the intersection of the vas deferens and the seminal vesicles. This ring-shaped organ adds fluid to the semen and along with muscles nearby is responsible for squeezing the semen and sperm into the urethra during **ejaculation** (e-JACK-yoo-LAY-shun), the release of the semen and sperm from the body. Because sperm and semen travel out of the body through the urethra, it is part of the male's reproductive system as well as the passageway for liquid waste or urine.

Male Reproductive System (internal view)

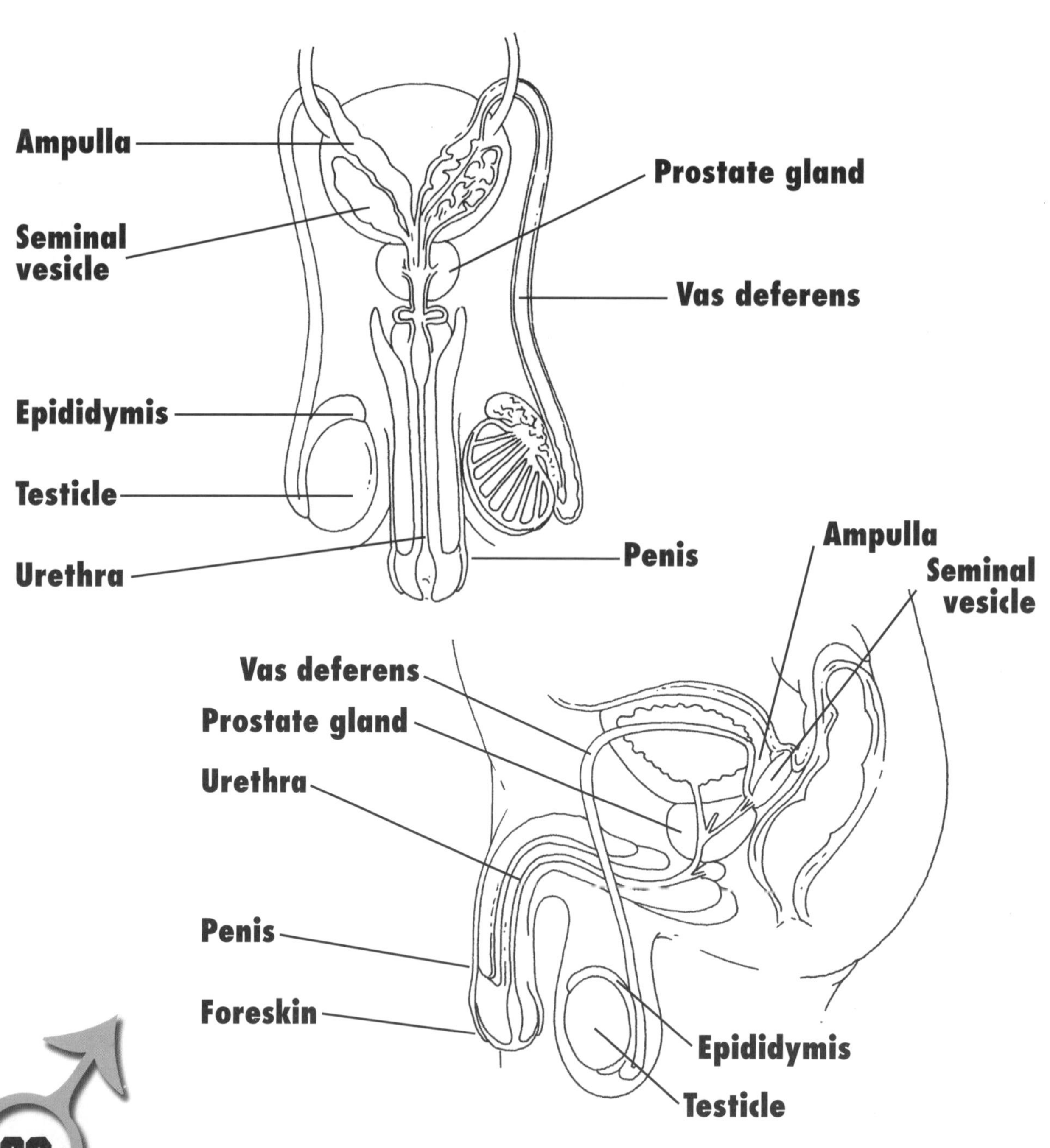

Remember that we've used the word "genitals" or "genitalia" for the area of the body below the abdomen or belly and between the legs for both males and females. For girls, the specific word is **vulva** (VUL-vuh) for the female genitals. For girls, it's much more difficult to actually see their vulva, so a small mirror makes it easier for a girl to see and understand this part of her body. At the center of the vulva is the opening to the **urethra** (yoo-REE-thruh), the passage that allows urine to be released from the bladder. Below the urethral opening is the opening to the **vagina** (vuh-JIE-nuh), the elastic, muscular passageway that leads to the internal reproductive organs.

Surrounding the opening to the vagina are two thick folds of skin called the outer **labia** (LAY-bee-uh), a Latin word meaning "lips." A second set of folds of skin, the inner labia, are inside the outer labia.

The most sensitive part of the vulva is the **clitoris** (KLIT-uh-ris), a small cylinder-shaped organ located where the labia meet at the top of the vulva. "Sensitive" in this case means that it responds to touch or stimulation. The clitoris, though small, is largely responsible for making sexual intercourse pleasant for the woman. (Sexual intercourse will be described in Chapter 5.)

Another part of the vulva, present when most (but not all) girls are born, is a thin layer of stretchy tissue located around the opening to the vagina called the **hymen** (HI-muhn). It is about the thickness of plastic wrap and may look like anything from a half moon (the most common), to a thin film with one or more small perforations (holes), to a spider web. Very, very seldom does the hymen completely cover or block the vaginal opening. Typically, the hymen is worn away by general physical activity—probably more quickly as a result of vigorous athletic activity or stretching movement. In the past, people thought that evidence of an intact hymen proved that a female had not had **sexual intercourse.** But we know today that most hymens start to wear away simply with the passage of time.

The word **virgin** (VUHR-gin) once referred to young unmarried women. It was assumed that these young women had never experienced sexual intercourse, so "virgin" was understood as a girl or woman who had not had intercourse. Today the word "virgin" is used for anyone—male or female—who has not had intercourse.

Female Reproductive System (external view)

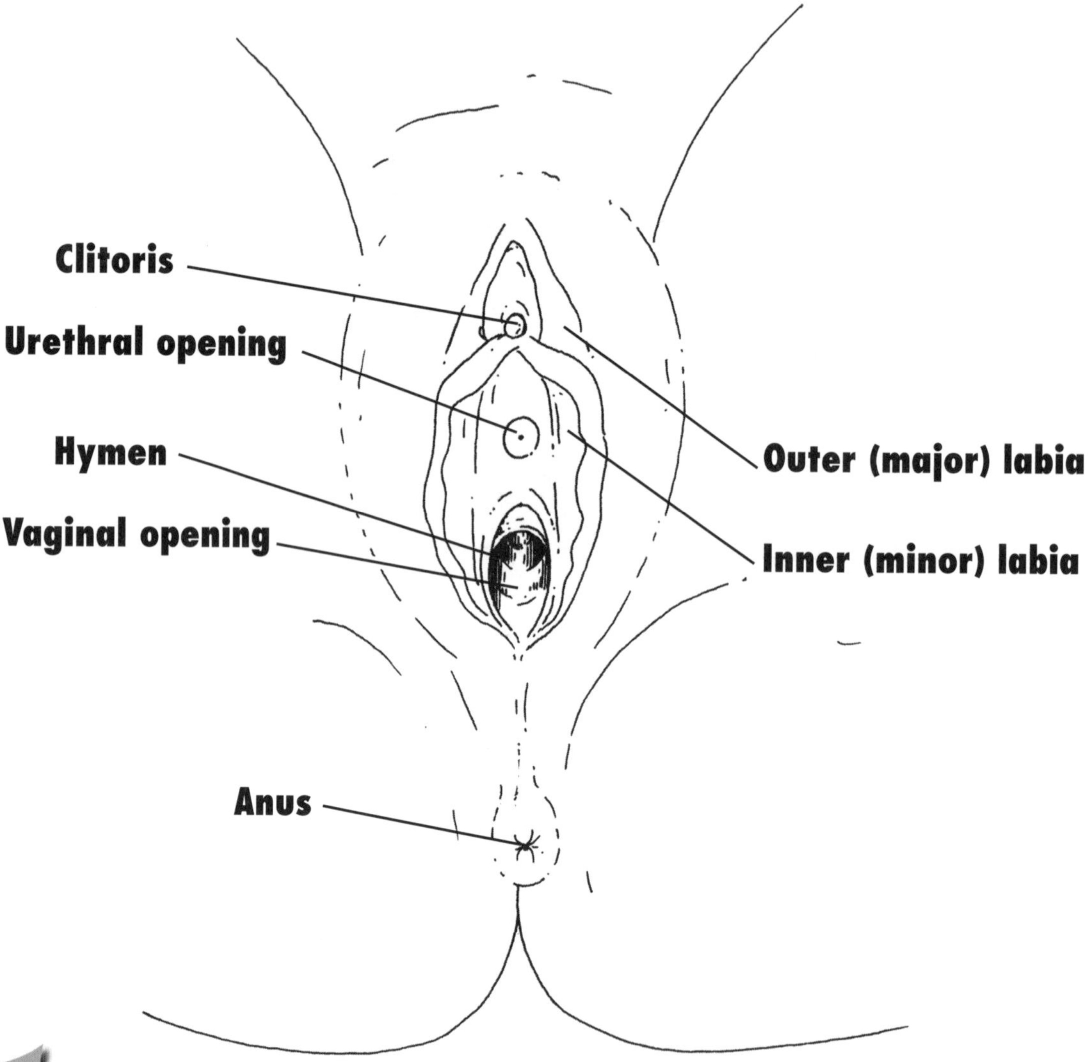

Female Reproductive System (internal view)

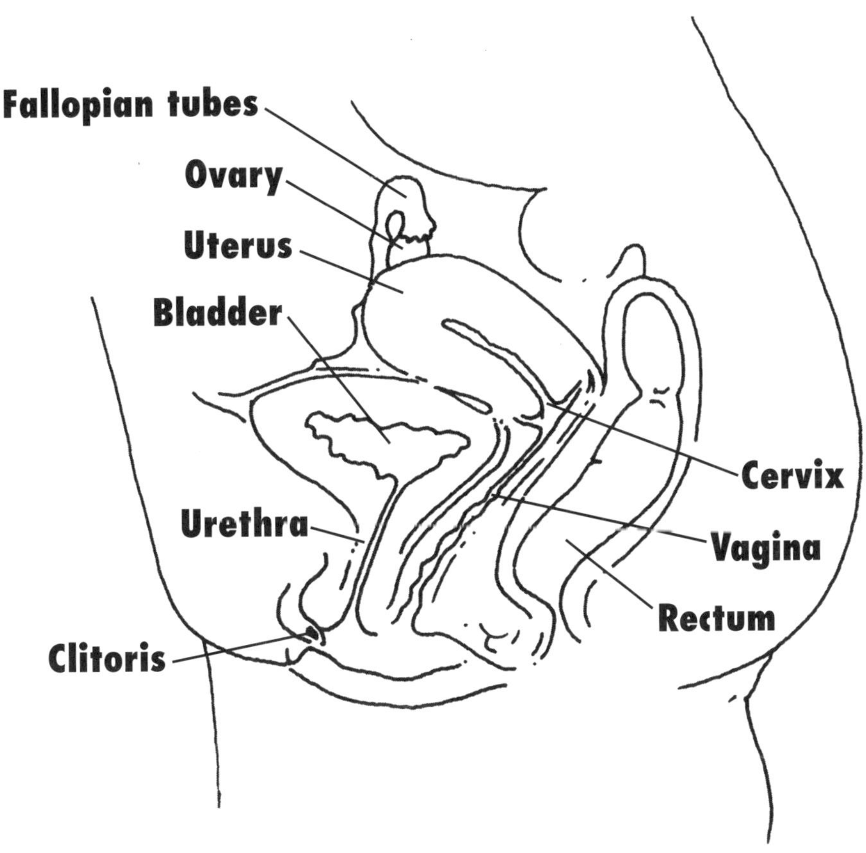

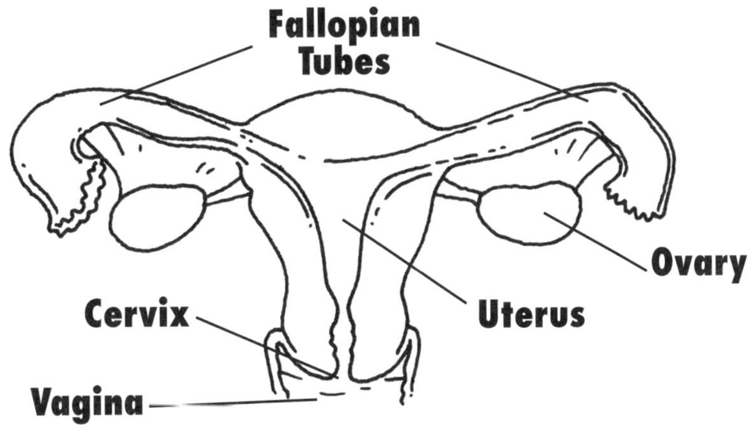

What incredible bodies God has given us! And our bodies work in wonderful ways, especially the internal sexual reproduction system, which is made up of the organs inside our bodies. We've described the outer genitals, or outer parts. Now on to the insides.

The **vagina,** an elastic, muscular passageway that starts at the vaginal opening, leads to the other internal sex organs and looks much like a long, deflated balloon. About three to five inches long when fully developed, the vagina has amazing stretch-ability. It can stretch enough to receive the erect male penis during sexual intercourse or to allow a baby to travel out of the mother's body during childbirth. (More about that in Chapter 5.)

The vagina connects to the **uterus** (YOO-ter-us) or **womb** (WOOM), a hollow organ located inside the lower abdomen. The uterus, shaped like a light bulb or an upside-down pear, is where a baby can grow and develop if a female becomes pregnant. Although normally no bigger than a tightly closed fist, during **pregnancy** (PREG-nun-see) the uterus stretches to make space for the baby growing inside. The **cervix** (SER-viks) is the lower part of the uterus that extends into the vagina. The lining of the uterus is called the **endometrium** (ehn-doh-MEE-tree-uhm).

The **fallopian tubes** (fuh-LOH-pee-uhn), about four inches long and as thick as a strand of cooked spaghetti, branch out from either side of the upper part of the uterus. They are lined with tiny hairs, **cilia** (SILL-ee-uh). At the fringed or finger-like ends of the fallopian tubes are the **ovaries** (OH-vuh-reez) two almond-sized organs located a little lower than the waist. Stored in the ovaries are thousands of **ova** (OH-vah), or female reproductive cells. Each **ovum** (OH-vum—the singular form of ova), about the size of the point on a sharp pencil, is inside a tiny sac called a **follicle** (FALL-uh-kuhl). The ovaries, like the testicles in males, produce those chemicals called hormones.

OPPOSITE SEX

 Other, Not Opposite

You probably hear the words "opposite sex" very often. But let's think before we use them. We are all created by the same God. When you add arms, legs, shoulders, and other bodily parts, you can see that males and females have more body parts in common than ones that distinguish us as male and female. You can see that God made us to complete the human race, to "go together." God made us special in differing ways that, together, make for wonderful human beings, all valued and loved.

Jesus taught that the barriers that we imagine exist between people do not come from God. He stood firmly against all of the things that are believed to make one group of people the opposite of another. This is certainly true for males and females who are not, by any stretch of the imagination, opposites.

The Apostle Paul wrote, "There is no longer Jew or Greek, there is no longer slave or free, there is no longer male and female; for all of you are one in Christ Jesus" (Galatians 3:28).

We are different, of course, but definitely not opposites.

That's quite a vocabulary lesson so far! You can expect that learning some of those words and their meanings will eventually help you better appreciate this wonderful body of yours, created in God's own image. With our expanded vocabulary, we're ready to learn about what happens to our bodies during that period of amazing change called adolescence. And what happens is nothing short of awesome!

> **There is no longer Jew or Greek, there is no longer slave or free, there is no longer male and female; for all of you are one in Christ Jesus. (Galatians 3:28)**

37

Words, words, and more words—so many to remember and so many that sound so strange! It's like learning a foreign language—always awkward at first, but as you practice saying words out loud, it gets easier. Of course, there are slang terms that many kids use, sometimes without knowing what they mean. With the new information you have, you can know the proper words and their meanings, making you a better communicator and making you much more confident.

Here is a list of words from this chapter. See if you can identify those that are specifically female or male parts or are parts everyone has. Put a check in the correct box — the one with the female symbol (♀), the male symbol (♂), or both.

	♀	♂	♀♂		♀	♂	♀♂
abdomen (26)				ovaries (36)			
anus (26)				penis (29)			
cervix (36)				pregnancy (36)			
cilia (36)				prostate gland (31)			
circumcision (29)				puberty (25)			
clitoris (33)				scrotum (30)			
cremaster muscle (31)				seminal vesicles (31)			
ejaculation (31)				sexual			
endometrium (36)				intercourse (33)			
epididymis (31)				shaft (29)			
fallopian tubes (36)				sperm (30)			
foreskin (29)				testicles (30)			
genitals (26)				urethra (26)			
glans (29)				uterus/womb (36)			
hormones (30)				vagina (33)			
hymen (33)				vas deferens (31)			
labia (33)				virgin (33)			
ova/ovum (36)				vulva (33)			

For the answers, check the page number listed with the term.

Chapter 3

Making Our Way Through Puberty

40

When will I start to change?

How fast—or how slow—will the changes happen?

When will it all be over?

Am I normal?

For everything there is a season, and a time for every matter under heaven. (Ecclesiastes 3:1)

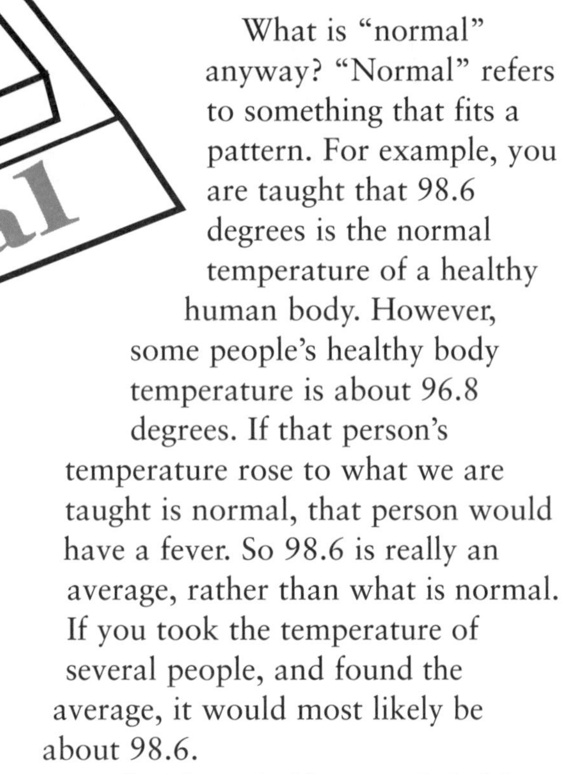

What is "normal" anyway? "Normal" refers to something that fits a pattern. For example, you are taught that 98.6 degrees is the normal temperature of a healthy human body. However, some people's healthy body temperature is about 96.8 degrees. If that person's temperature rose to what we are taught is normal, that person would have a fever. So 98.6 is really an average, rather than what is normal. If you took the temperature of several people, and found the average, it would most likely be about 98.6.

So it's probably more helpful to talk about averages. If Roslyn has her first period when she is eleven, and Lucy has her first when she is fifteen, the average of the two is thirteen. But which one is normal? If Gary starts shaving when he is eighteen, and Russ starts when he is fourteen, which of them is normal? NOW HEAR THIS! All of them are normal, and so are you! How you are growing and developing represents your personal normal.

When will you start the changes of adolescence? How fast will it happen? When will it all be over? The answers to these questions are locked up in your **chromosomes** (KROH-muh-sohmz). The center of each cell in your body, like the cells of all plants and animals, contains chromosomes. These tiny rods transmit characteristics from parent to child. That's called **heredity** (huh-REHD-uh-tee). Chromosomes also determine which **gender** (JEN-der) we are—male or female. Structures called **genes** (JEENZ) are located in specific positions on the chromosomes. They determine what characteristics—such as height and skin, eye and hair color—are inherited from parents, from grandparents, and from all ancestors.

While factors like climate, diet, and health can influence our growth and development, mostly our genes determine when you will start, how quickly you will go through, and when you will be finished with puberty. "Puberty" comes from a Latin word that means "to be covered with hair." It refers to *the time during which one's body changes from that of a child to that of an adult* — including when new hair grows in previously hairless places.

Glands and Hormones

Your body contains a variety of small (sometimes tiny) fluid-producing organs called glands. The fluids produced by some glands are ones you can see—sweat and saliva, for instance. Others, called **endocrine** (EHN-doh-krihn) **glands**, send their fluids directly into the bloodstream. Another is the **pituitary** (pih-TOO-uh-tare-ee) **gland** located behind your eyes at the center of your brain. The fluids produced by these glands are the chemicals called **hormones** mentioned in Chapter 2. Think of hormones as the *body's chemical communication system*, taking messages from one part of the body to another through the bloodstream.

The pituitary gland begins manufacturing hormones a few years before anyone notices. When the pituitary hormones get to the ovaries in females and testicles in males, the reproductive glands begin producing hormones of their own and the adolescent marathon begins!

These hormones signal the body that it is time to change from girl to woman or boy to man.

Two Halves of the Human Race

Since we live in a world where there are two genders, it makes sense for us to understand both halves of the human race. Boys who know about girls' bodies and girls who know about boys' bodies are going to be more respectful of the other gender. Sounds just like what God had in mind for these "in God's image" creations. So let's learn about each other, these wonderful creations!

The Five Stages of Puberty in Girls

Notice the differences between the girls illustrated on pages 66, 67, and 68. When it comes to puberty, every girl's body (just like every boy's body) is unique. At the time that is right for the individual, the pituitary gland sends its hormone signals to the ovaries, instructing them to produce more **estrogen** (ESS-truh-juhn), the hormone responsible for the changes that mark puberty in girls. Let's look carefully at the five stages.

<u>Stage 1</u> (age range, 8–11 years; average age, 10 or 11)
While there are typically no external signs of development during Stage 1, girls' pituitary glands begin producing more hormones—sending stronger signals. Upon receiving the message, the ovaries get larger and begin producing more **estrogen** (ESS-truh-juhn), the hormone that causes female sexual development during puberty.

The illustrations on pages 66, 67, and 68 show four girls at eleven, sixteen, and twenty-one years old. Look again at the differences between the girls. As their bodies develop, none of them begin or end at the same place, nor do they get from start to finish at the same rate. The one consistent thing is that hormones prompt the changes as girls grow older.

- pituitary glands produce hormones
- no externals signs
- ovaries larger
- ovaries produce more estrogen

<u>Stage 2</u> (age range, 8–14 years; average age, 11 or 12)

During Stage 2 girls often experience their growth spurt, making many of them taller than boys of their age. Although boys and girls begin to mature about the same time, girls generally begin their time of faster growth about two years before boys. Note that not all bones grow at exactly the same rate, which means that arms, legs, and feet typically spend time looking a bit out of proportion to the rest of the body. And, in preparation for possible child-bearing, the hips of the girl get wider, giving her a more female shape.

Pubic hair (PEW-bick) appears above the vulva and on the edges of the labia and signals that puberty has begun. Pubic hair functions like eyelashes, preventing dust or dirt particles from irritating this sensitive part of the body.

The growth of underarm hair and the darkening and growth of hair on the legs is another sign of puberty. While in many cultures hair on legs and underarms is acceptable and desirable, in our country females generally remove that bodily hair through shaving or other means. Girls will want to talk with their mothers or other family members about their response.

The **breasts** begin to develop during Stage 2. The first sign of change might be the presence of a small, button-like lump behind the **nipple** or center of the breast, and the increased sensitivity of the nipples. Even though the breasts have not increased much in size, many girls choose to purchase and begin wearing their first bra about this time. That bra helps reduce the irritation from clothing rubbing the nipples. The darker circle around the nipple is called the **areola** (air-ee-OH-lah).

While in childhood the breasts are generally flat, during puberty the breasts begin to swell. Inside the breasts are 15 to 25 sections called **lobes,** where milk is produced when (and not until) a woman has a baby. While breast feeding, the baby sucks on the nipple, which causes the milk to travel from the lobes through channels called **milk ducts** (duhkts) to the nipple. During puberty, a girl's breasts are developing so that she might later be able to breast feed.

Breast Development: Owner Beware!

Breast development—its starting point, how long it lasts, and how much development occurs—differs greatly among growing girls. Girls whose breasts develop early may feel self-conscious. Girls whose breasts develop later may feel self-conscious. Because such a big deal is made about breasts in the media, girls may think that they should be concerned about the size of their breasts. KNOW THIS: All breasts, small or large, are normal, and work the same way, the way that God intended.

Beware of advertisers and the media waiting to take advantage of girls who feel insecure about their bodies. These people hope to sell creams, machines, medications, exercises, and surgeries that are supposed to change the appearance of breasts—to make them more like what they are saying is normal or more desirable. Remember: Who's normal? You, that's who! You are fine exactly the way God has made you.

> - growth spurt
> - widening of hips
> - appearance of pubic hair, underarm hair
> - darkening of hair on arms and legs
> - beginning breast development

Female Breast

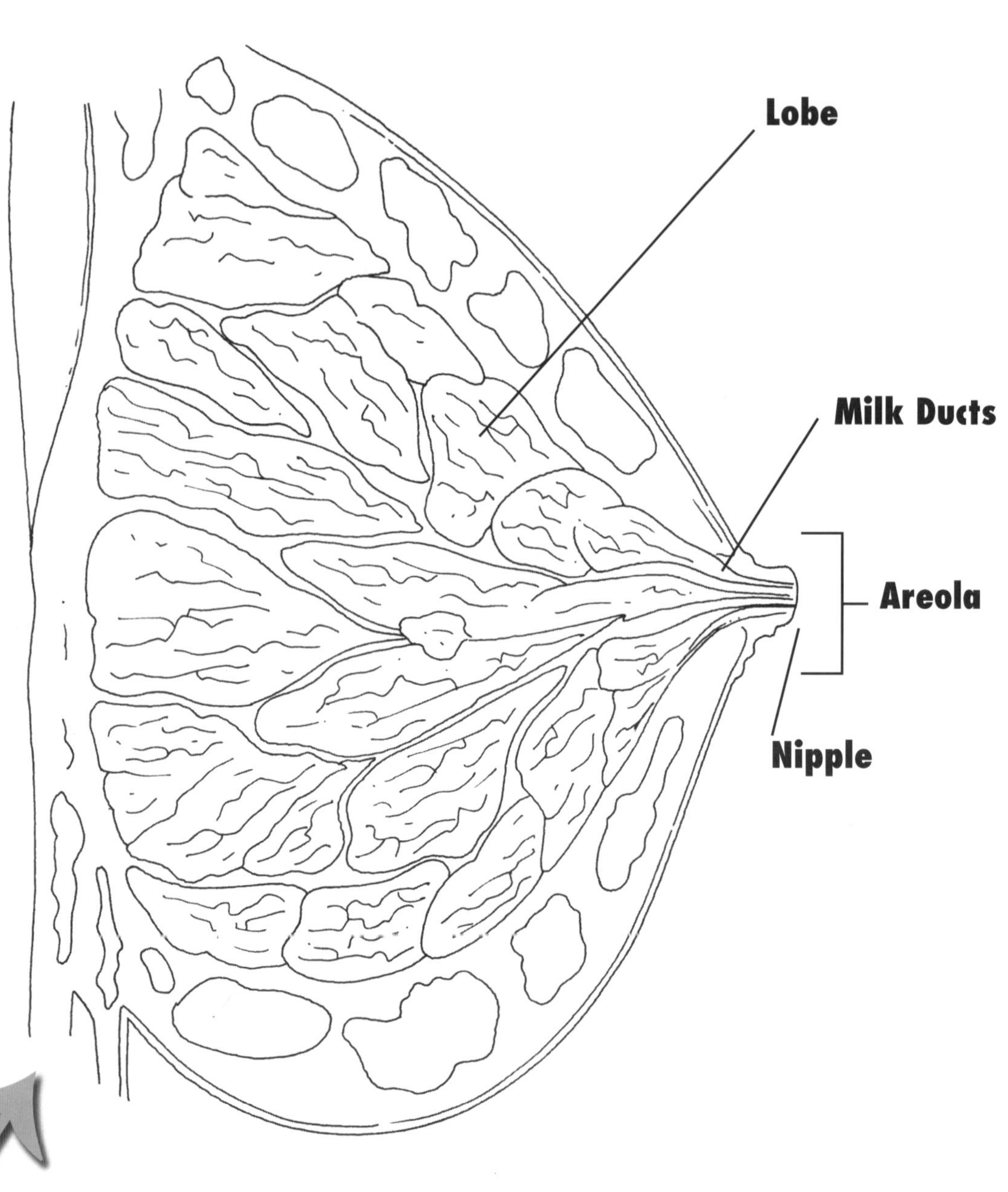

<u>Stage 3</u> (age range, 9–15 years; average age, 12 or 13)

As breasts continue to develop, that dark circle around the nipple gets even darker and larger, the pubic hair gets thicker and curlier, and the body continues to grow.

Stage 3 can be a busy time! Girls at this stage often notice a clear or whitish discharge in their underwear, coming from the vagina. Yes, it's normal. God has designed the female body with the ability to cleanse itself. The uterus and vagina produce fluids that wash away dead tissue cells and keep themselves clean. That discharge, when first noticed, can be a sign that a girl is about to experience her first period, which is given that name because it happens periodically rather than constantly.

More on periods a little later.

BSE: Breast Self-Examination

Once a girl has begun having periods, a regular (monthly) **Breast Self-Examination (BSE)** is essential in order to be alert to changes that could signal possible breast disease. Regular exams will help a girl find her personal normal when it comes to her breasts. Breasts are normally lumpy, so regular exams are the only way to be able to identify a condition that needs to be reported to a parent or to the doctor. Without an awareness of what is normal, the abnormal may not be recognized.

Because the breasts retain fluid and are more sensitive during a period, it is best to do a BSE right after each month's period. It involves looking at the breasts to be aware of any changes in skin or shape and checking for an irregular discharge from the nipples (not all discharges are a problem.) A thorough self-exam, best done when lying down, includes feeling the entire breast and the area around the breasts, all the way down to the chest wall.

Breast Exam

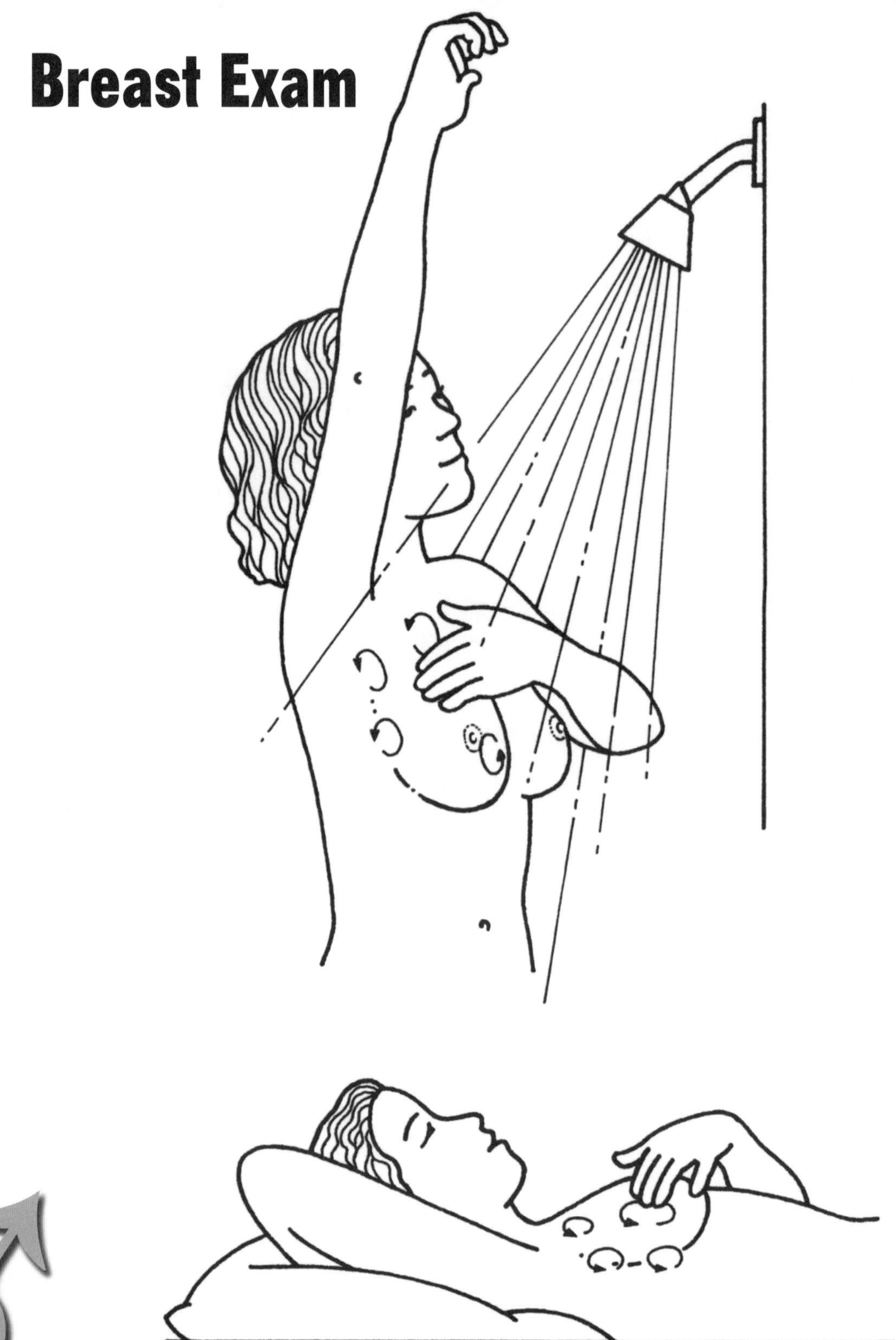

50

1. Hand behind head to stretch out the breast tissue.
2. Press firmly all around the perimeter of the breast and work your way to the nipple in a spiral motion.
3. Feel underneath the arms for unusual lumps in the lymph glands area.
4. Repeat with the other breast.

What is being looked for? Something that wasn't there during the last exam. It might be a hard, pea-sized lump—one that doesn't "give" when pressed. But anything suspicious needs to be reported immediately. Thousands of women are diagnosed with breast cancer each year. Early detection and treatment can prevent death in many cases.

> - continued breast growth, areola darker and larger
> - pubic hair coarsens and darkens, still sparse
> - body growing
> - growth of vagina and uterus
> - clear or whitish discharge from vagina
> - menstruation possible

<u>**Stage 4**</u> (age range, 10–16 years; average age, 13 or 14)

The vulva basically transforms during Stage 4. The outer and inner labia darken and become thicker and more wrinkly. During this stage, the hymen, if it is still present, grows thicker.

Another change is the increased sensitivity of the genital area. What does sensitive mean? Although the vulva has always been sensitive to touch, during puberty it responds more strongly with pleasant tingling sensations. Girls may discover new sensations if they use their hands to explore the vulva—especially the clitoris, which grows larger during puberty, and the vagina. The touching or stroking of the genitals is a self-discovery process of all girls and boys. This kind of touching is called **masturbation** (MASS-ter-BAY-shun).

Puberty is a time when girls find that the nice feelings caused by genital touch when they were younger have been replaced by much stronger feelings. The amount of blood flowing to the genital area increases, causing the labia and the clitoris to become much more sensitive when stimulated. Because masturbation is an activity for both males and females, we'll discuss it in more depth in Chapter 6.

That Time of the Month

A cycle is something that happens over and over again. Like the revolutions of the wheels on your bike or the beat to your favorite song, the female body has its own rhythm or cycle: the **menstrual** (MEHN-stroo-uhl) **cycle**. The estrogen produced by the ovaries signals the body to begin the cycle between the ages of ten and sixteen, but it can be earlier or later.

A girl is born with hundreds of thousands of **ova** (or microscopic "eggs") in her ovaries. Each **ovum** (OH-vum—the singular of ova) is about the size of the point on a sharp pencil. As puberty begins, the ova begin to change and mature, and move toward the surface of the **ovary**. The ovum is released from the ovary about every 28 days and the process is called **ovulation** (ah-vyuh-LAY-shun).

The ovaries generally take turns ovulating—the right ovary one month, and the left ovary the next. Once the ovum has been released from the ovary, tiny hairs called **cilia** (SILL-ee-uh) then wave the ovum through the four-inch-long fallopian tube at about one inch per day! Just before ovulation, the lining of the uterus (the **endometrium**)

doubles in thickness with new blood vessels and spongy tissue—all rich with nutrients. If, after sexual intercourse, the ovum traveling through the fallopian tube combines with a sperm (the male reproductive cell), the fertilized ovum implants in the endometrium where it is nourished, and the new life begins. More often than not, there is no fertilization, the ovum and a sperm do not combine, and the ovum disintegrates. Within a few weeks, the uterus sheds the endometrium as a discharge of blood and tissue that passes through the vagina and out of the body. This whole process is called **menstruation** (mehn-STRAY-shun) or simply the **period,** since it happens periodically. Lasting typically four to seven days, or an average of five days, females use either absorbent pads called "sanitary napkins" inside their underwear or "tampons," which are absorbent material inserted into the vagina, to hold the one-quarter to one-third cup of discharge over the course of the period. Using tampons does not mean that girls are no longer virgins and no, the tampon can't go into the uterus.

<table><tr><td>GETTING STARTED   Here's some info you need to know:</td></tr></table>

- Periods may be very irregular (occurring every 20 days to 3–4 months) at the beginning.
- Bathing and washing are especially important during menstruation. Change the tampon or napkin regularly.
- Menstruation isn't a disease. You can do all your normal activities, although you may have some cramping.
- Menstruation is normal, but it's not always convenient; girls can't tell exactly what day their "period" will start. Being prepared is always a challenge.

Most Months

Just before and during a female's "period" (the time of menstrual discharge), she will often be irritable or extremely emotional. The hormones that control menstruation are flowing throughout the body and can impact the brain and emotions. We call this time the **Premenstrual Syndrome** (conditions just before one's "period") or **PMS**. If the symptoms become particularly severe, a doctor's attention may be needed. This is a time for her friends and family to be understanding.

Do women continue to menstruate their whole lives? The answer is no. **Menopause** (MEHN-uh-pahz) is when ovulation slows down and menstruation eventually stops, generally at around age 50. Once again, this is part of God's plan. Since sexuality does not depend on a person's ability to reproduce, women remain sexual beings after menopause.

<u>**Stage 5**</u> (age range, 12–19 years; average age, 15)
Girls: You may want to talk with your female relatives about when their first periods began, and about how they felt just before it happened. It will give you a clue about your own body's schedule.

> - adult body shape
> - complete breast development
> - full pubic hair
> - full height
> - monthly menstrual periods and ovulation

Notice the differences between the boys illustrated on pages 66, 67, and 68. When it comes to puberty, every boy's body (just like every girl's body) is unique. At the time that is right for the individual, the pituitary gland sends its hormone signals to the testicles, instructing them to produce more **testosterone** (tess-TOSS-tuh-rone), the hormone responsible for puberty in boys. Let's look carefully at the five stages.

<u>**Stage 1**</u> (age range, 9–12 years; average age, 10)

Boys at Stage 1 of puberty, like girls at the same stage, don't show much in the way of change. The pituitary gland increases its hormone production, and when those hormones reach the testicles, invisible changes happen.

Like girls, boys can be very self-conscious, concerned when the changes of puberty seem to come either too early or too late. They might not mind when attention is called to their achievements in other areas, but being noticed because their pants are too short or their voices are changing is not welcomed.

> - testicles developing
> - testicles produce more testosterone
> - few external signs
> - some start growth spurt

<u>**Stage 2**</u> (age range, 9–15 years; average age, 12 or 13)

Once boys begin to change in visible ways, they seem to make up for lost time, and those changes can happen very rapidly. It is not unusual for a boy to gain as much as 25 pounds in a year's time, and to grow six or more inches.

> - testicles and scrotum begin to enlarge
> - very little pubic hair
> - increase in height
> - change in body shape

<u>**Stage 3**</u> (age range, 11–16 years; average age, 13 or 14)

Stage 3 is when visible changes really start to happen for boys—like when the testicles and scrotum grow larger and the scrotum and shaft of the penis darken in color. With testicles growing larger, the need increases to protect them. Boys should never hit another boy in the testicles. In addition to causing severe pain, damage can be caused as well. Athletic supporters or cup protectors should be worn when involved in sports.

- testicles and scrotum begin to enlarge
- penis and scrotum skin growing darker
- penis grows in length
- pubic hair darker and coarser
- underarm hair
- height increase
- body face shape looks more adult
- voice begins to deepen and crack
- some hair around anus

Jockstrap

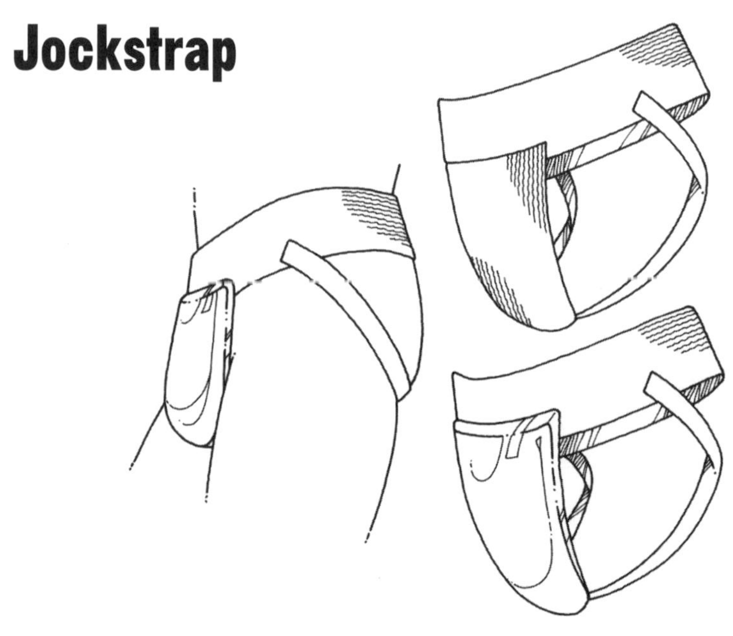

Testicular Self-exam

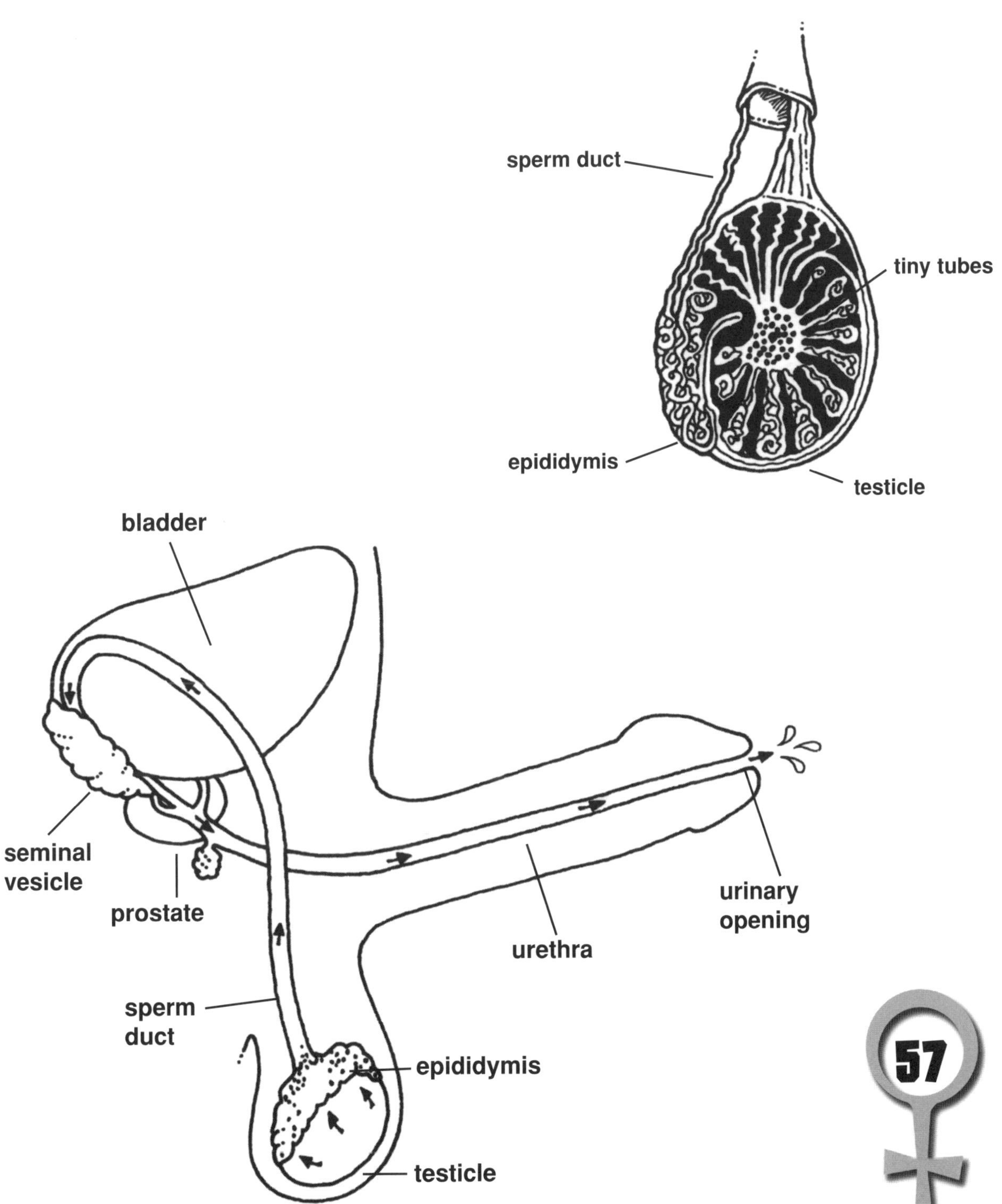

TSE: Testicular Self-Examination

The **Testicular Self-Examination** (tess-TIC-yuh-luhr) or **TSE** is checking one's testicles for lumps or irregularities, best done in the shower when the scrotum is warm and relaxed. Each testicle is rolled between the thumb and first three fingers, and the entire surface of the testicles checked. (See page 57. The sperm ducts and epididymis, connected to the testicles, don't count as irregularities.) All questionable lumps or changes should be reported to a doctor. Although testicular cancer accounts for only 1% of cancers in men, it is the most common form of cancer in males between the ages of 15 and 34, and it is becoming more common.

Does Size Matter?

During Stage 3, the penis grows longer. (Wider or bigger around comes later.) Since genital size is a concern for many boys (and many men), the following information might help: Penises are usually between three and one-fourth and four and one-fourth inches long when soft or limp, and usually between five and seven inches long when hard or **erect** (ih-REKT). We emphasize "usually" because we are talking about what is average—not about what is normal, what should be, or what makes someone more masculine or manly.

Does penis size matter? Based on magazines and the Internet, it would seem that it matters a lot to some people. Again, advertisers are eager to take advantage of a male's insecurity over the size of his penis. They offer medications, machines, surgeries, exercises, and creams that are "guaranteed" to increase penis length, make erections firmer or last longer, and generally improve sex life. Not only do these products not work, some can do lasting damage to the genitals.

While <u>penis size doesn't make a difference</u> in how masculine you are or what kind of a husband or father you will be, it can make a difference in how you feel about yourself. We suggest right now, well before you know what your adult body will look like, that you remind yourself on a regular basis that you are God's outstanding creation— just the way you are and just the way you will be.

58

Stage 3 is also about pubic hair that gets darker, thicker, and begins to claim more territory, spreading out from its initial site above the penis and on the scrotum. Hair also begins to grow in the underarms, and hair on the rest of the body begins to get thicker and darker. Some boys will have enough facial hair to start shaving, but we'll discuss that as part of Stage 4.

The voice begins to deepen, but not without its share of cracks and squeaks. The voice box is growing, and the muscles responsible for producing sound need to be retrained. In the meantime, don't "force" your voice. Be sure to breathe before you speak. This won't eliminate the sometimes embarrassing squeaks, pops, and cracks, but may minimize them.

<u>**Stage 4**</u> (age range, 11–17 years; average age, 14 or 15)

At Stage 4 the penis is getting wider or bigger around, and the testicles and scrotum continue growing. For the first time the testicles begin producing sperm, the male reproductive cells—in the neighborhood of *20 million* of them per month once full maturity is reached. Sperm production slows down as men get older but can continue to some degree for the rest of their lives.

Over fifty percent of all boys experience some swelling and tenderness of the **breasts** during puberty. The nipples may get a bit larger, the ring of colored flesh around the nipple may get wider and darker, and many boys notice a rather flat, button-like lump under one or both nipples. This is neither a sign of disease nor an indication that one is turning into a girl! It is one of the ways in which boys' bodies react to hormones. All bodies have both estrogen and testosterone. The estrogen is responsible for breast development, but there is not enough of it in guys to cause their breasts to fully develop. Hormones need a chance to get balanced. Once that happens, this condition passes.

This is probably a good time to remind you to be sensitive to what girls are going through regarding breast development, and NEVER to tease girls about their breasts.

In Stage 4, boys begin to experience more frequent erections. Most of the time, the penis is **flaccid** (FLA-sid) which means soft or limp. Sometimes, though, as a result of stimulation, blood rushes into the sponge-like tissue of the penis, filling the spaces inside the shaft. Muscles at the base of the penis tighten and keep the blood from

flowing back into the body. This causes the penis to become larger, firmer, and to stand out from the body—sometimes straight up, sometimes straight out, sometimes somewhere in between. Everyone's angle is a little different. This is an erection, and it occurs in males of all ages, even before birth.

The stimulation that leads to an erection can be caused by touching the genitals, being rubbed by tight clothing, needing to urinate, feeling the vibrations of a car or bus that needs new shock absorbers, having thoughts about sex, or simply being close to a person for whom one has special feelings. Boys and men experience erections several times while they are asleep and often awaken with an erection.

Sometimes erections happen with no obvious explanation. A boy might be thinking of just about anything and suddenly have an erection. Adolescents react more strongly than children to what they see, hear, smell, taste, feel, and think. You used to look at a rock and see a rock. Now you might see that same rock, be reminded of someplace special you once visited, and begin to have some of the same feelings you had during that visit. Your mind brings those feelings back automatically. Such connections could be the reason behind the for-no-reason erections that boys experience more frequently during puberty.

Erections usually aren't noticed by anyone else and don't last forever. Should a boy find himself with an erection at a time when someone might notice it—whether that be in the locker room or in the middle of giving a report in front of the class—he needs to remember that what he is experiencing is perfectly normal. Focus on something else (not sexual thoughts) and the erection will subside soon. Relax, it's normal. The good news? On the other side of adolescence, hormones calm down—and so do erections.

You have probably seen the advertisements and heard about drugs that men take when they are having just the opposite problem—when they can't have an erection and are unable to have sexual intercourse. However, men who don't need these drugs also are taking them out of curiosity or thinking that their enjoyment of intercourse will be increased. Very bad idea.

- penis width and length increases
- testicles and scrotum keep growing
- testicles begin to produce sperm
- pubic hair of adult texture now
- areola darkens; some boys experience swelling / tenderness
- sensitivity of genitals
- more frequent erections
- first ejaculation
- facial hair on chin and upper lip
- voice deepens
- skin gets dry

The First Ejaculation

The first ejaculation is another mark of Stage 4. Hormones have signaled the body to begin producing the sperm and semen. **Ejaculation** (e-JACK-yoo-LAY-shun) refers to when the mixture of sperm and semen is pushed from the seminal vesicles into the urethra and out of the body. As those muscles plus the prostate gland automatically give a strong squeeze, the fluid is squirted out of the penis. This ejaculation is accompanied by an **orgasm** (OR-gaz-uhm), which, as with girls, refers to very pleasant pulsing feelings in the genital area.

Two out of three boys experience their first ejaculation during masturbation—the deliberate rubbing or stroking of one's sex organs. As boys' genitals become more sensitive during puberty, masturbation produces very strong and pleasant sensations. More on this later.

One out of three boys has his first ejaculation while he is asleep. This is called a **nocturnal emission** (nock-TER-nul-ee-MISH-uhn), or wet dream. The seminal vesicles are full of semen, the vas deferens is full of sperm, and a boy's dreams may be full of sexual thoughts— enough to lead to an orgasm. This is not an act the boy can control. Guys cannot deliberately have a wet dream, or keep from having one. It is involuntary. It's okay to have them, and okay if you don't. This is normal, and part of God's plan.

If you are a boy and you awaken and find a stiff dry spot or a damp spot on your pajamas or sheets, you'll know what happened. Don't worry, just toss your clothing or sheets into the washer. Boys who experience nocturnal emissions need to know that parents—both dads and moms—understand

Time to Buzz the Fuzz?

Boys are often anxious to shave for the first time. Some twelve-year-olds will find that they need or want to begin shaving—upper lips and chins seem to be the first targets. Others won't need to start until sixteen, seventeen, or even later. It's helpful to talk with a parent or other adult about when and how to shave.

<u>Stage 5</u> (age range, 14–18 years; average age, 16 years)

Stage 5 is the time for fine-tuning all the growth and changes that have been happening, although many males continue to develop and grow taller into their twenties. This varies a great deal. Guys, you may want to ask your male relatives when they reached their full height, when they began shaving, and so forth. That will give you a clue about your own possible development.

- nearing full adult height and physique
- adult appearing pubic hair and genitals
- facial hair, shaving soon
- continuing to grow taller and develop more body hair, especially chest hair

For Both Girls and Boys

We were created
and are being created by God:
some of us female,
some of us male,
each of us special,
each of us sexual,
each of us growing at our own unique pace.

Puberty and Personal Hygiene

You may notice that your underarms have begun to perspire more and that the odor has changed. This may be true for other parts of your body—your hands, feet, and genitals—as well. These are effects of the hormones at work in your body. Regular bathing or showering and changing clothing daily are important, plus you now should use a deodorant or antiperspirant as well as possibly foot powder. A word about deodorants: they are not a substitute for bathing or showering! When your family says to you, "It's time to take a shower," listen to them!

Acne

Oily skin and **acne** (ACK-nee) is another common condition of puberty. Yes, pimples, zits, whiteheads, and blackheads can be blamed on the hormones too! What to do about them?

There is no guaranteed prevention or cure for acne. Zits can appear anywhere on the body, especially on the face, shoulders, back, and chest. Popping them or picking at them can make them worse and leave you with unwanted scars.

Practice the best hygiene you can, but also be prepared to accept that for most young persons, acne comes with hormones and puberty. While some adults continue to get acne, it generally isn't to the degree that they experienced as teens. If you are worried about acne becoming a problem, talk with your physician about it.

- Get lots of sleep.
- Drink lots of water.
- Eat healthy.
- Keep hair clean and away from face.

You need more rest than you think. Adolescent bodies are working overtime to make the transition from child to adult. Those changes take energy. Besides bodily changes, you are experiencing changes in your life like new responsibilities, additional school work, or more sports. Friends take energy too.

Experts say that tweens need between nine and ten hours of sleep each night. Staying up late for a few nights with the plan to catch up on the weekend won't work. In addition to your body's need to rest, your brain needs the time you're asleep to rest too. Adolescents who don't get enough sleep are often irritable, impatient, and even inappropriately aggressive.

* * * * * * * * * * * *

This whole journey through puberty started with the work of that special timing mechanism, the pituitary gland, and the hormone signals it is sending through your body right this very minute. Pretty amazing, God's plan! It's all normal—and so, by the way, are you!

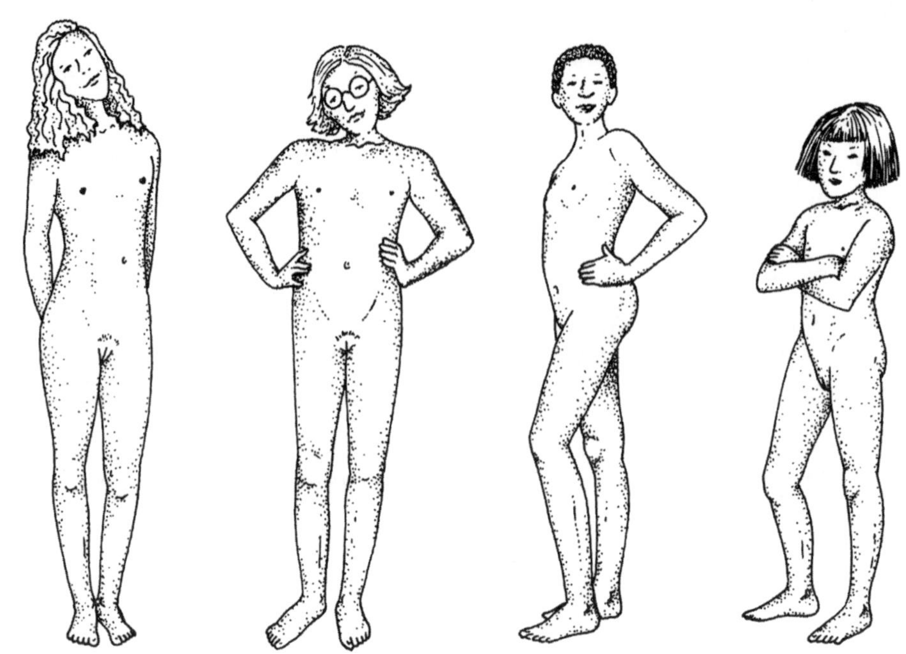

Around 11 Years Old

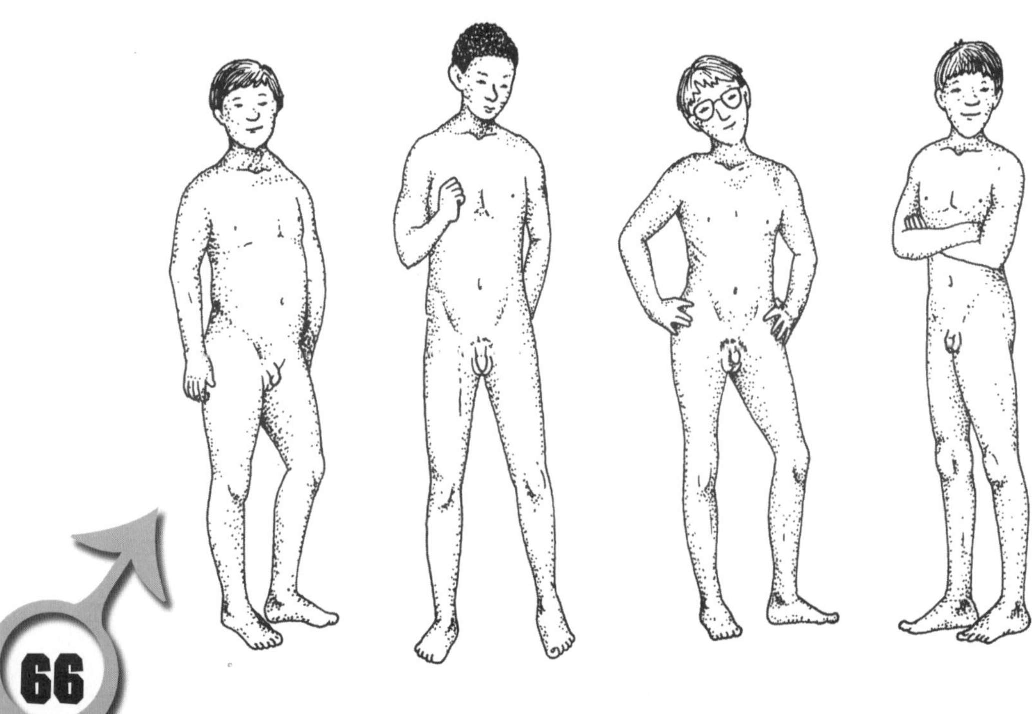

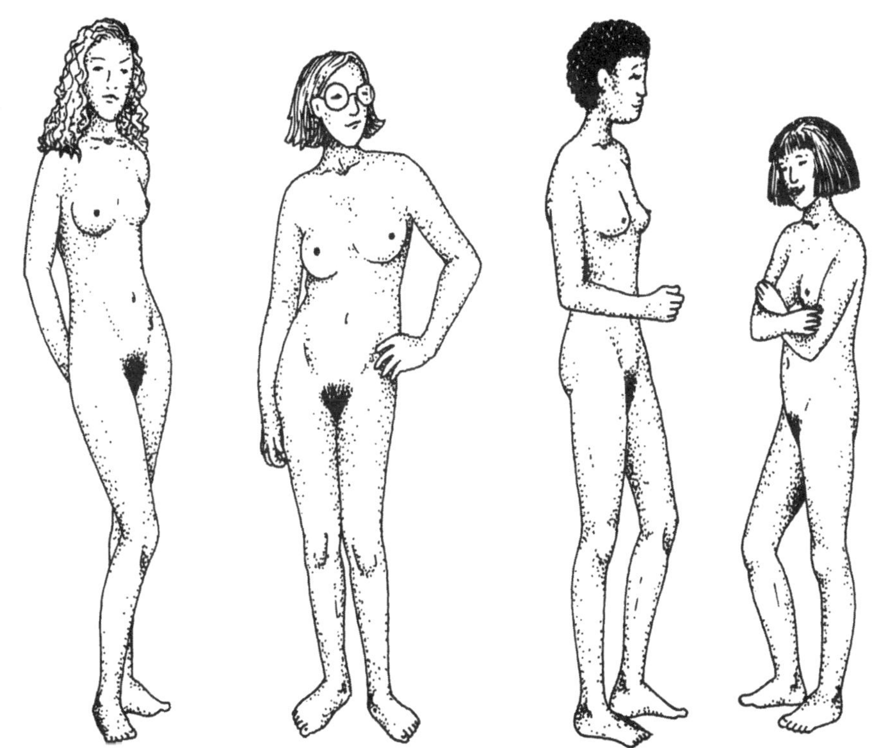

Around 16 Years Old

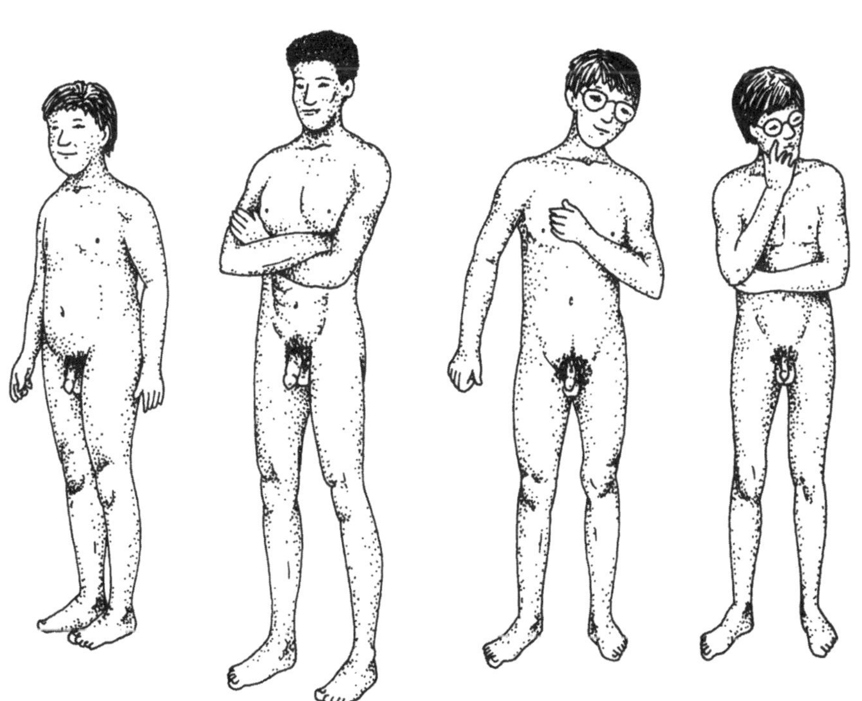

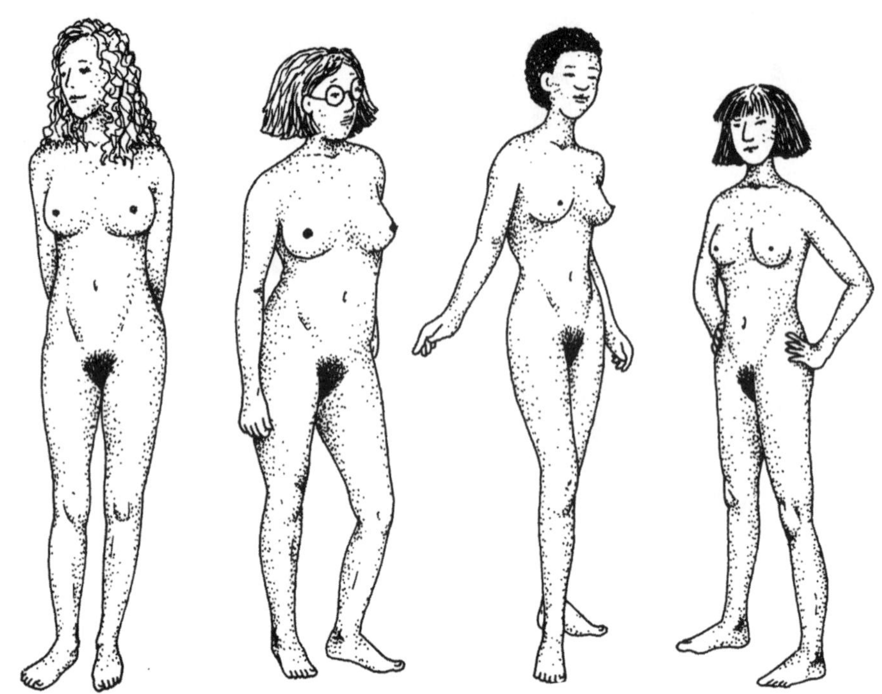

Around 21 Years Old

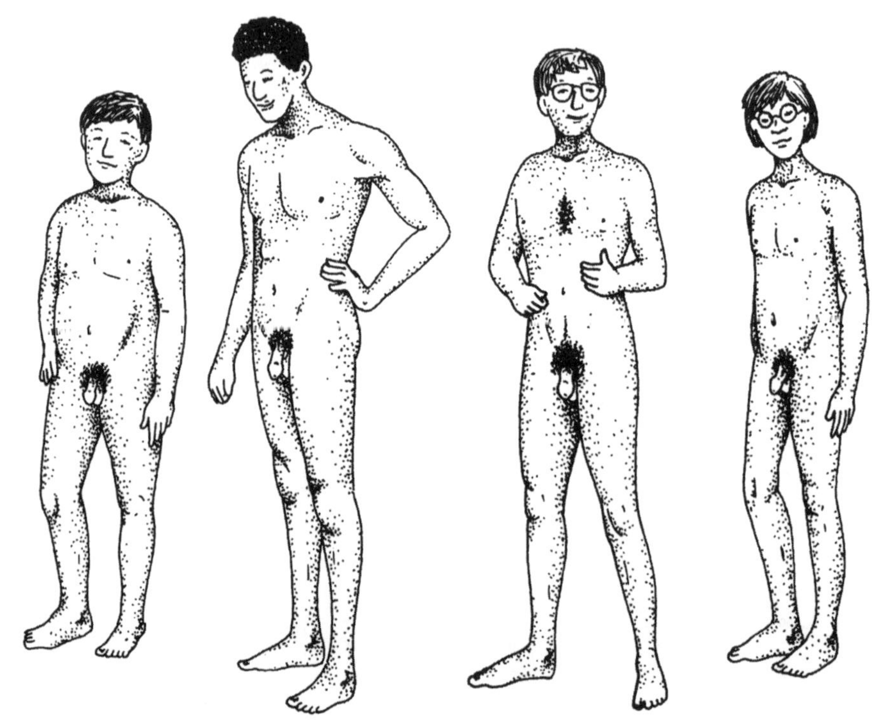

Chapter 4

Created by God for Intimacy

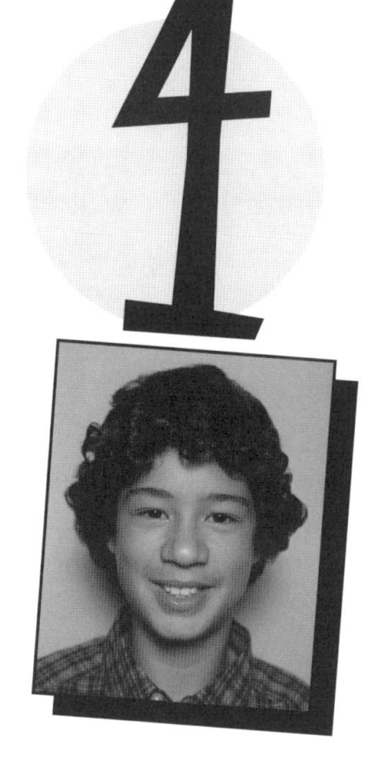

69

Starting With Adam and Eve

Read Genesis 2:15-25

The story of Adam and Eve is a story of people growing up and growing in relationships with others and with God. Long before it was written down, this tale was passed from one generation to the next by storytellers. Reading the story in Genesis 2:15-25, we hear the storyteller almost chuckle while explaining God's solution to Adam's need for companionship: Get him a pet!

"So, Adam, what are you going to name all of these critters?" Naming the animals kept Adam busy for a while, but it wasn't long before God (and Adam) realized that, nice as the animals were, they didn't meet Adam's need for a partner. Adam needed another human being—someone with whom he could actually carry on a conversation.

So God created Eve, the first woman. Eve was human, but she was a different kind of human—the female kind. Perhaps that's what made Eve a suitable partner for Adam! They enjoyed the ways they were the same and also enjoyed discovering and exploring the many ways in which they were different. Differences gave them something to talk about!

You may have trouble picturing two naked people just sitting and chatting. But the Bible says that this was true for Adam and Eve, "naked and not ashamed" (Genesis 2:25). Their differences—including their body parts—were no problem. They were God's creations—comfortable with themselves, comfortable with each other, and comfortable with God. It was all good.

Unfortunately Adam and Eve didn't stay comfortable and things didn't stay good. They made poor decisions, disobeyed God, and their relationship with God and with one another began to fall apart. Nakedness and their differences were suddenly an issue, and they quickly covered their bodies. When Adam and Eve gave in to temptation, their relationship with God broke down; their differences became an embarrassment to them. They lost the intimacy, both with God and with each other.

Intimacy is:

Friendship
Cooperation
Comfort
Communication:
  talking
   and
   listening
Compassion
Caring
Honesty
Openness
Trust
Confidentiality
Selflessness
Laughter
  and tears
Time
Respect

Somewhat like Adam and Eve allowed their actions and their differences to break their intimacy, so the growth process causes the differences among boys, among girls, and between girls and boys to be noticed. It's easy for young people to begin moving apart from each other. Comparing themselves to others, they decide who is better. That's called competition. Competition calls for winners and losers.

But there is another way, described by the word intimacy. Maybe **intimacy** (IN-tuh-muh-see) isn't a new word to you. You may have heard it in relation to sexual behavior between men and women—sexual touching or intercourse, for example. But intimacy is much more than close contact between bodies. It means a close relationship, a growing and deepening friendship. Look at the cone here to see the varieties of intimate relationships.

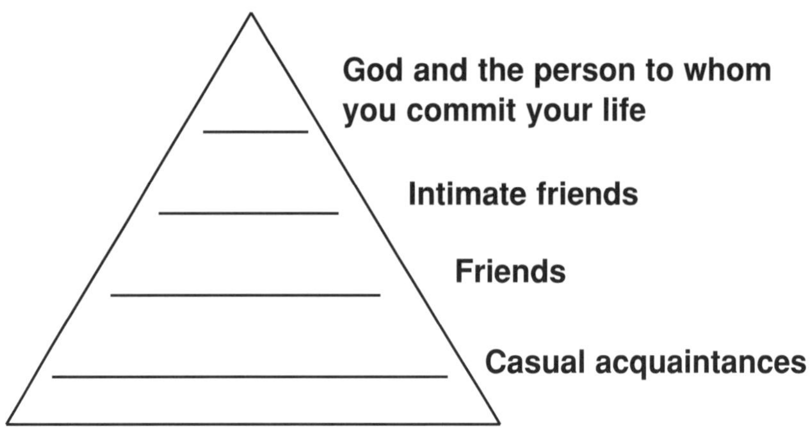

You'll see the degrees of intimacy, starting with our casual friends. You can also see really focused intimacy—with God and with one's spouse. How does this happen?

What are the basic similarities between growing intimacy with God and with other people? Intimacy happens when persons spend time together, when they take time to get to know each other: what each likes, dislikes, hopes, and fears, and when they learn to accept one another just as they are. Intimacy can happen with God or between any two people who are willing to work at it.

Intimacy describes the relationship that puts an end to competition. The object of intimacy is not to decide who is best, but to simply enjoy being together, knowing each other well, and accomplishing together—

cooperatively. Intimacy is the basis of close friendships, and ultimately, the basis for love—among friends and between a husband and a wife.

Love captures many of the other words connected to intimacy—selflessness (God's love for the world led to the gift of Jesus, the only Son God had to give), vulnerability, commitment, and respect, for example. Love is not just something we feel for another person, it is about the way we treat that person. Love in action says

You don't have to be exactly like me
in order to be a worthwhile person
or in order for me to care about you.
You are God's good creation just the way you are.

We live in a society that teaches us to take care of ourselves first. For Christians, Jesus is the model that shows us total selflessness—just the opposite. He put the needs of others before his own, which is the message of the Cross. Christian selflessness exposes us to the possibility of being hurt. Intimacy can be scary because it exposes our **vulnerability** (VUHL-ner-uh-BILL-uh-tee), which is a weakness or obstacle we can't overcome. Just like Superman and other "super heroes," we all have our vulnerabilities—fears, things we either can't do or will never do well—especially not all by ourselves. Boys can't be girls or know what it feels like to be a girl. Girls can't be boys or know what it feels like to be a boy. We can only understand each other by getting close to those persons who have experienced it firsthand. Our need for others makes us vulnerable, and that does allow the possibility that we could get hurt. But because God has created us for relationships and their blessings, we take the risk.

So you're asking, "What does this have to do with SEX?" This: Our sexuality points to our attraction for relationship with others and for physical connection with someone of the other gender for love and for creating new life. The more we know about our sexuality, the better our relationships will be, and the happier we'll be!

God's desire is for us
to live in an intimate relationship
with God and with one another.

When you feel positive about yourself—including about your growing and changing body—you find lots of energy and enthusiasm for loving God and loving neighbor. You're all set to get at the task of building bridges—building intimacy—between people and between people and God. This positive sense of self has a lot to do with how you see yourself as a female or as a male. It doesn't happen automatically; instead you have to work at it. I can't think of more important work for girls and boys like you to be doing.

Bridge-building begins by learning about yourself. You're learning to call the parts and functions of your body by their proper names. You're learning to recognize some of the slang terms that are used to describe the same parts and functions. You don't have to use the slang terms, but you'll be more confident if you know what they refer to. It's usually best to have a bit more information on hand than what you actually need.

Your expanded vocabulary will make it easier for you to talk to others about the thoughts and feelings you have about yourself. You'll also be able to better understand others. You are building bridges with words, information, and understandings that you have in common.

It is important that girls build bridges with other girls. There are some things that only another girl can completely understand. Boys need to build bridges with other boys. Many people live with the stereotype that boys and men never share their feelings, that they can work out all of their problems on their own. Not so! Boys need to practice talking to each other about their feelings.

Girls and boys get to know each other by talking to each other. This particular kind of bridge-building can prepare people for the possibility of being married someday. But whether or not they choose to be married, boys and girls need to build bridges while they are young, simply because they live in a world where people come in two genders! These stories may help you to see how important bridge-building can be.

FRIENDS: Paula and Tiffany

Paula and Tiffany had a problem! As their bodies began to change, they found that their nipples were becoming sensitive and were being irritated by the rubbing of their clothing. Their breasts hadn't developed much—at least they hadn't gotten that much larger, and they were sure that their mothers wouldn't see the need for them to begin wearing bras.

They suffered separately for a while. Finally, Paula timidly mentioned the situation to Tiffany. Both were relieved to know that they weren't alone with the problem.

"I can't believe you've been going through the same thing!" Together they came up with a plan. "If one of us can get her mother to agree to the bra, the other's mother is sure to go along with the idea!" They decided that at 5 o'clock they would both go to their mothers, tell them that they would like to shop for a bra, and mention the fact that they were both talking to their mothers at that very moment.

To their amazement both mothers understood and agreed to a mother-daughter night out with all four of them, to include shopping for their first bras. Let's give those mothers some credit for remembering back to when they experienced the same thing. But let's also recognize two smart friends who managed to put their feelings into words and who tackled their problem together!

FRIENDS: Susan and Ronny

"Valerie Taylor likes you!" shouted Susan to Ronny as he headed toward home. Ronny turned, gave her a dirty look, and kept going.

"Ronny, did you hear me? I said Val—"

"Heard you?" he interrupted. "The whole neighborhood heard you!"

"Sorry. Well, do you like her?"

"Like who?"

"You said you heard me! Valerie Taylor!"

"I did hear you!"

"But you still didn't answer me."

"I don't plan to."

"You make me so angry!" said Susan.

"You embarrass me," Ronny replied.

"I didn't think you could embarrass."

"Surprise!"

Susan thought for a moment. "I'm sorry, Ronny. I guess I wasn't thinking."

I don't know where Valerie Taylor stands, but if Ronny and Susan can keep talking and listening and can be more sensitive to each other, they might even become friends!

FRIENDS: Martin and Randy

Martin and Randy, two twelve-year-old friends with heads full of stereotypes (see page 78) as to what twelve-year-old boys ought to look like, are in the locker room after swim practice. As they stand under the showers, Martin is aware that his body hasn't started to develop yet—at least not on the outside where others can see. (By the way, Martin isn't the only one making such observations! It's just one of the things that growing boys and girls do.) Martin hasn't started to sprout any hair under his arms or around his genitals—quite normal for his age. Randy, on the other hand, is showing some of the signs of puberty, including the start of a moustache—also quite normal.

"Martin, do you think I need to shave this moustache?"

"What?"

"Do you think this moustache makes my face look dirty?"

"I don't know. Not dirty. Though it's hard to miss."

"Yeah. You're lucky. No one stares at your upper lip and giggles."

"I guess not. But I'll bet you aren't handed a kid's menu at restaurants."

"You're right about that. But I'd rather not have people looking at me. It makes me feel like I'm abnormal or something."

"Really? I figured people were looking at me because I'm abnormal—not a single hair anyplace other than on my head."

"Nah. You're normal."

"So are you."

"I think you just might be right."

Breaking Stereotypes

Originally, **stereotype** (STAIR-ee-uh-type) referred to a molded metal plate with words or pictures on the surface used in the printing process to print words repeatedly. Today we use that same word to describe how all people of a particular group are sometimes expected to look, or behave, or think, allowing no room for individuality. It suggests (inaccurately) that if you know one category a person fits into, you know everything about that person. For example, you might think (wrongly) that persons of a particular cultural group are all alike, or all Christians are alike, or all males are alike. Those are stereotypes.

A stereotype of males or of what it means to be **masculine** (MASS-kyuh-lin) might suggest that all men are young, muscular, tall, and handsome. They wear certain clothes, have their hair styled the same way, use the same phrases, and love playing football. A stereotype of females or of what it means to be **feminine** (FEHM-uh-nin) might try to convince us that all women are thin, young, and have well-shaped bodies. They always wear just the right shade of nail polish, lipstick, and eye makeup. They are never seen in the same outfit twice in one month, they love to cook, and they're afraid of spiders.

Even though these stereotypes do not describe all men or all women—or even most of them—there are advertisers spending millions of dollars every year to convince us that everyone ought to fit these stereotypes. Their goal is to convince us that we fall short of the ideal and that their product is just what we need to be "real men" or "real women." Their objective is to make money by causing people to feel insecure, especially about their bodies. Next they offer us the perfect solution to that insecurity: Buy my product and you'll be more like the male or female that everyone should want to be. DON'T BELIEVE THEM!

Breaking stereotypes sets you free—free to be and to celebrate who you are, because that's the way God created you!

People often affirm the appearance or behavior of young girls by making comments such as "She's such a little lady!" The same happens to young boys with comments like, "He's all boy!"

People may mean well, but they aren't always helpful. Little girls are little girls—not women. It's not fair to expect a little girl to be a woman and to miss being a little girl. Boys don't come just half boy. But people have a picture in their minds—a stereotype—of what girls and boys should be like. When they see things in girls and boys that match their mental pictures, they point these things out. What happens then? Boys and girls grow up thinking that all boys should be alike and that all girls should be alike. That's neither true nor fair.

As you have a better understanding of your body and others' bodies, you're developing your understanding of what it means to be **feminine** (FEHM-uh-nin) and **masculine** (MASS-kyuh-lin). Think about Martin and Randy, the boys in the last story, or of Cindy and Dawn, two girls at a sleepover, who have their minds filled with stereotypes. Cindy was ten years old when she had her first period. At twelve she is one of the girls whose breasts are well-developed. Dawn is three months older than Cindy but still hasn't had her first period and hasn't started wearing a bra yet. Neither Dawn nor Cindy represent the stereotype for twelve-year-old girls. Neither one is more feminine than the other.

When it comes to gender, you're either male or female; you're either a boy or a girl. Gender is not something you have by degrees. You can't be more girl or less girl, or more boy or less boy, than someone else. We've already mentioned chromosomes, and Chapter 5 will explain a bit more how gender is determined. What you need to know in this chapter is that you are either all one or the other—all male or all female.

Feminine is something different. So is masculine. Despite what our culture teaches, they have nothing to do with how early you develop, how late you develop, or the size of your body. Femininity is how a female chooses to express her understanding of what it means to be female. Masculinity is how a male chooses to express his understanding of what it means to be male. Different persons express themselves in different ways. Some of us will choose to express our femaleness or

maleness in traditional, culturally defined ways. That's fine, but it's also fine to choose not to be limited by what people have considered feminine and masculine in the past.

 Freedom

You're free to decide for yourself. You may want to be like someone else, but you don't have to be like anyone else. You can feel great about being who you are! Let's go a step further. Feeling positive about yourself is your right and your responsibility as a child of God. A story from the life of Jesus might help us understand.

Jesus was once approached by a scribe, (a teacher of religious law) who asked him, "Which commandment is the first of all?" Jesus answered the question by quoting from the Book of Deuteronomy. "'Hear, O Israel!' Jesus said. 'The Lord our God, the Lord is one; you shall love the Lord your God with all your heart, and with all your soul, and with all your mind, and with all your strength.'" Jesus didn't stop there. He took what he considered to be the most important commandment and paired it with a second one: "'You shall love your neighbor as yourself,'" Jesus said to the scribe. "There is no other commandment greater than these" (from Mark 12:28-31).

As you mature, you are discovering that your feelings about God, about other people, and about yourself are all connected. If you aren't positive about yourself, it's pretty tough to put your whole self—heart, soul, mind, and strength—into loving God. If you haven't learned to love yourself, to say to yourself, I'm OK the way I am, the way God made me, you're going to have a tough time loving your neighbor. Remember that "neighbor" can refer to anybody—not just the person who lives next door, or even the person who is like you in many ways. If you're a girl, the kind of neighbor Jesus talks about could very well be a boy. And if you're a boy, it might be a girl!

Today girls and boys may have similar dreams and share many of the same possibilities. Girls and boys both have opportunities to receive an education. Both take part in athletics, baby-sit, bag groceries at the supermarket, mow the lawn, prepare meals, and wash the dishes. "That's a boy's job" or "Only girls do that" are comments from another era. And that's a good thing.

Many of the stereotypes are gone. Boys and girls are becoming aware that, first of all, they are persons. Gender need have no influence on decisions they make about who they are and about what they will become. Questions such as What kind of work is right for a man? and What kind of work is right for a woman? are being replaced by What do I enjoy doing? What am I good at? What kinds of work would I rather avoid? What things frighten me? What sacrifices am I willing to make in order to reach my goals? and What needs are there in the world and how might God be calling me to help meet those needs?

You're free to follow God's call for your life in any way!

Chapter 5

Creating With God

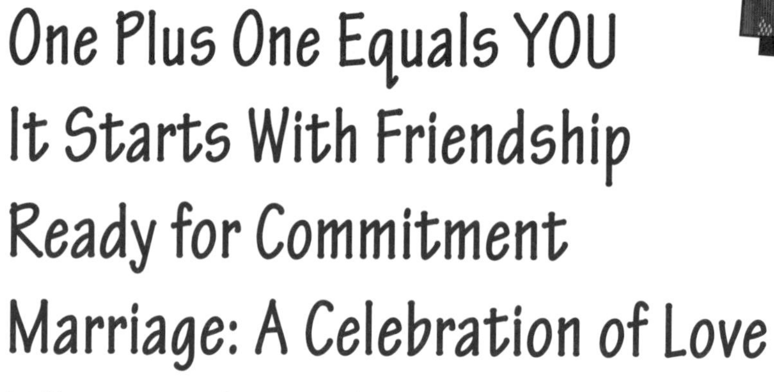

One Plus One Equals You

Several years ago, the union of one cell from a male (your father) and one cell from a female (your mother) resulted in something completely new and unique—YOU!

> So God created humankind in God's image,
> in the image of God, God created them;
> male and female God created them.
> (Genesis 1:27, adapted)

Read Genesis 1:27

The verse above repeats the same idea three times, saying that God created us, not in some random way, but in God's image. How awesome! This "image" is of God's character and being, not, of course, God's physical image, since God is spirit.

The ability to create new life is an amazing gift from God, one in which your parents were able to share as they, with God, created you. That amazing gift of creating life, and the gift of being male or being female, are now your gifts, and are mysteries you can spend a lifetime exploring and enjoying.

As you grow and develop through puberty, you might think, "now that I'm going through puberty, I'm becoming a sexual being!" The truth is that you've always been a sexual being. You were destined for maleness or femaleness from the moment those two cells got together—from the moment of your **conception** (kuhn-SEP-shun). Your body began responding in sexual ways even before you were born. Doctors tell us that even in the womb, males' penises become erect at times and females' vaginas produce special fluids. Such responses do not necessarily mean that a person is thinking about sex or feeling sexy (Before birth? Of course not!), just that the person is a sexual being, whose body responds in male or female ways.

And now, entering puberty, your distinct maleness or femaleness really begins to show and your interest in "the other sex" grows. That's God's plan!

"The opposite sex" is a phrase you may hear, but it's one you won't find in this book except at the beginning of this sentence. Being male does not make one the opposite of being female, or the reverse. Being human gives us so much in common, regardless of our gender, that there's no way for us to be "opposite." Think of it this way: males and females complete God's design for wholeness. We need each other, relationally, and to create new life, physically.

As an adolescent moving into puberty, you will begin to have increased interest in the other sex. You will find that you like being with others—quite a change from just a few years before when boys and girls often want nothing to do with each other! Probably starting with group events, teens then begin to date, and later to enjoy the closeness of holding hands, dancing, hugging, and kissing.

Even more important they begin to tell each other about their hopes, their dreams, and their concerns—stuff that they don't share with just anyone. This is the growing intimacy that we discussed in Chapter 4. The key part of this beginning intimacy is more about talking than touching. Remember too that becoming "best friends," whether same-sex or romantically with the other sex, doesn't happen in a day. It takes time to build a friendship!

Such young persons are discovering that despite physical differences, persons of the other sex can understand their personal thoughts and feelings. While they have been learning about commitment and loyalty through same-sex friendships, they now see commitment and loyalty from a new perspective—from the perspective of the other gender. They learn to communicate in new ways—through smiles, gentle touches, and being close. These are experiences that prepare young people for lasting relationships.

Adolescent friendships are often intense, consuming, and emotional experiences—in part because adolescents tend to experience everything in intense, consuming, and emotional ways. But these relationships are valuable experiences that help young people grow emotionally and practice responsible decision-making. They help you discover and test out new emotions and help you get to know the special adult person you are in the process of becoming.

Ready for Commitment

In time most people find someone with whom they want to share their lives. They dream and make plans for a life together. They talk about sharing experiences and possessions and, in many cases, plan for the shared experience of parenting. They make a commitment to each other—a commitment of fidelity (faithfulness) through marriage, with the understanding that such a commitment will strengthen them individually and strengthen their ability to reach out to others. Good marriages make for happy lives and a healthy setting to raise children.

What can I do to make the one I love happy? is an important concern of husbands and wives. They learn that being faithful, honest, and open are some of the keys. They discover the joy of giving and receiving, the joy of exploring all the interesting things about another person. While they respect the ways in which each is different and allow each other the freedom to follow individual interests, they remain committed to the relationship. They laugh together and cry together. They talk to each other about what they are feeling and what they believe. Each person learns to make the marriage their first priority. The love they feel at first grows stronger as they meet the challenges of their life together.

Marriage: A Celebration of Love

Therefore a man leaves
his father and his mother
and clings to his wife,
and they become one flesh.

(Genesis 2:24)

Marriage is not for sissies, for the immature, or for the selfish. It is for two persons ready to commit their lives to each other for the rest of their lives, to share the joys and work through the difficulties. When two people love each other and blend their lives in a marriage, they express their love in many ways. A part of marriage is the joy of sharing physical love in **sexual intercourse.** (There are situations—during illness or as a result of physical or emotional limitations—when couples are unable to have sexual intercourse. Such couples discover other ways, through touch and being close, to express tender feelings for each other during that time.)

Stimulating touch, leading up to sexual intercourse is called **pleasuring** or **foreplay** (FOR-play). Foreplay can be thoughts of anticipation, loving words and touches, and kisses. These actions do not always have to lead to sexual intercourse, but can be demonstrations of love alone. Sexual intercourse is one important way in which husbands and wives celebrate their love, friendship, and commitment. That's why it's called "making love." The frequency of sexual intercourse varies greatly between couples, and in different times of their lives. Health, tiredness, and the amount of stress in their lives can affect how often a couple makes love. Couples will find what feels right for them. Know that married persons continue to be sexually active throughout their lives. That means your parents too, and likely your grandparents. And that's a good thing.

The physical expression of love in marriage is celebrated in the Bible in verses such as "Rejoice in the wife of your youth … may you be intoxicated always by her love" (from Proverbs 5:18-19) and "My beloved is mine and I am his" (Song of Solomon 2:16a).

In response to the pleasure of hugging and kissing and stroking each other, the male becomes sexually excited and his penis becomes erect (hard and enlarged). With sexual excitement for her too, the female's outer genitals swell, and her vagina becomes moist or lubricated. As their bodies rub together, pleasant feelings become very strong. At this time, the male puts his penis into the female's vagina. The peak of sexual excitement is orgasm—experienced by the male with ejaculation (the release of sperm and semen), and by the female as intense, pleasant pulsing of the vaginal walls and of the entire genital area. Some people describe these feelings as being something like a sneeze that builds and builds and finally explodes. Others say that an orgasm is like a wave washing over. Orgasm is the point at which the waves of feeling break over them. Following orgasm, the couple relaxes, and both have a sense of contentment. That's sexual intercourse.

And all of this is created by God!

How are babies made?

Don't worry. That's everyone's question. We've found that kids have bits and pieces of information, some accurate and some not-so-accurate, but they all want to know how it really works. So here goes.

It all starts with God. Read again the words from Psalm 139:13-16a.

For it was you who formed my inward parts;
you knit me together in my mother's womb.
I praise you, for I am fearfully
and wonderfully made.
Wonderful are your works;
that I know very well.
My frame was not hidden from you,
when I was being made in secret,
intricately woven in the depths of the earth.
Your eyes beheld my unformed substance.
(Psalm 139:13-16a)

And it—**conception**—or making a baby—is a special function of sexual intercourse (although it's not just for making babies!). The decision to have a baby or to be sexually active that can lead to pregnancy is a big decision that must be made carefully. In Chapter 2 we described how about every month an ovum is released from one of a mature female's ovaries into the fallopian tube. If that ovum joins with a sperm through intercourse, conception takes place, and a new life has begun.

Here's how that happens: Each time a male ejaculates, millions of tiny sperm are released along with the semen. The semen gives the sperm a major energy boost for the swim ahead. Each sperm is equipped with a tail to propel it from the vagina through the uterus, and through the uterus into the fallopian tube. Not all the sperm will

Sperm Meets Ovum

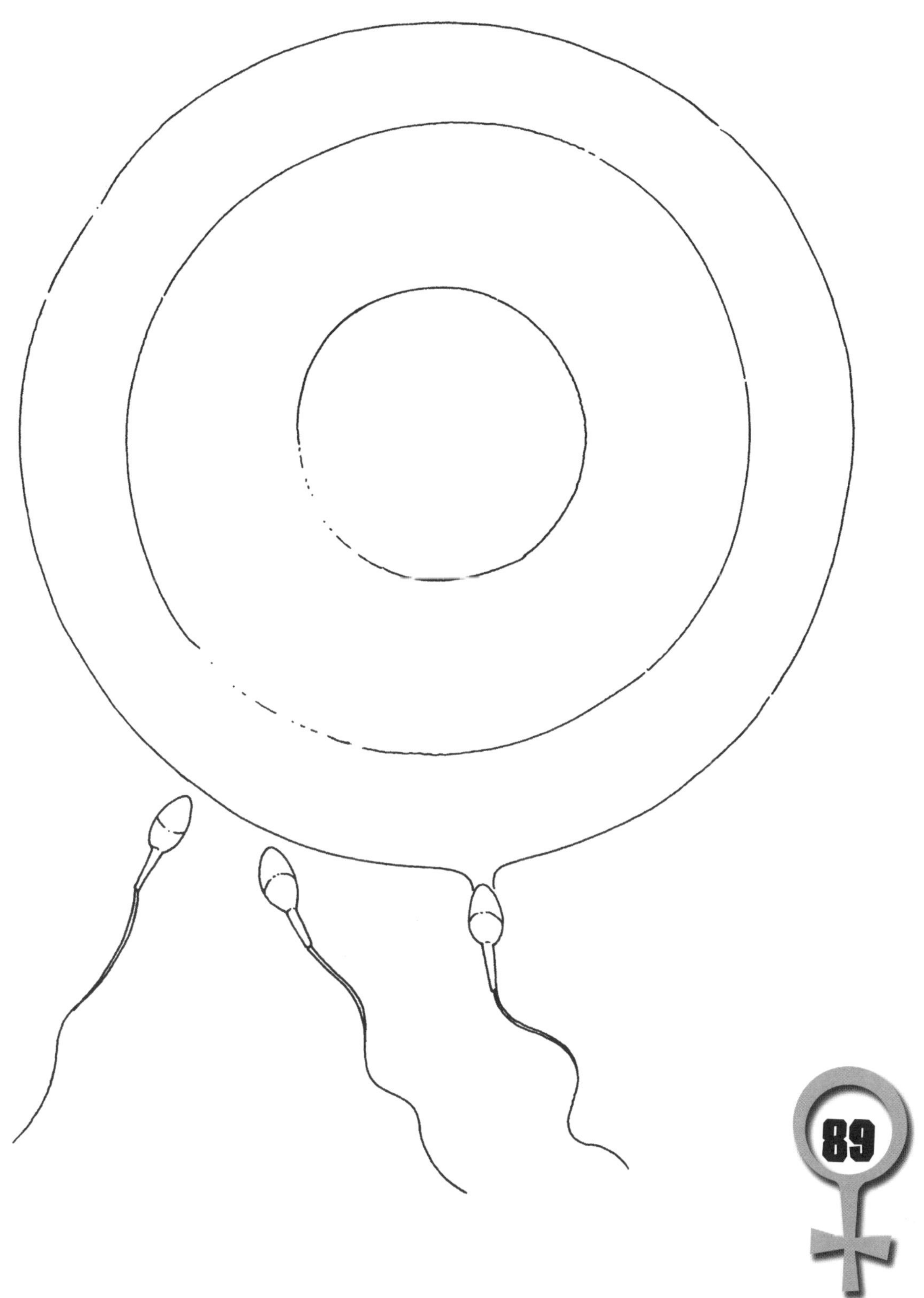

go the distance. Only the strongest will make it all the way, and the first one to reach the ovum and penetrate the outer shell is responsible for **fertilization** (FER-tuhl-uh-ZAY-shun). Immediately a chemical reaction takes place in that outer shell, and no other sperm can get inside.

At the moment of fertilization when the female and the male cells join, much is determined. In Chapter 3 we mentioned the genes that determine which traits you will inherit from your parents—hair, skin, and eye color; height; when and how quickly you will mature; and so forth. The genes are located on the chromosomes, which are part of every cell in your body.

Boy or girl? One of the chromosomes contributed by the ovum is an X chromosome. Sperm, on the other hand, can contain either an X or a Y chromosome. If the ovum is fertilized by a sperm with an X chromosome, the resulting XX combination will direct the development of a female. If the ovum is fertilized by a Y-carrying sperm, the XY combination will direct the development of a male. Lots more has to happen before the female and male organs develop, but the X and Y chromosomes get things moving in that direction.

Then what? The union of that ovum and sperm become a single cell, which then starts dividing and attaches itself to the wall of the uterus, where it grows and develops into the baby that is born approximately 40 weeks later. From about the tenth day following conception, the cluster of fast-growing cells begin to differentiate, meaning that the cells are no longer identical but are becoming specific body parts—heart, brain, lungs, and so forth. At three weeks, the **embryo** (EM-bree-oh) or developing baby at this stage is about one-tenth of an inch long. After three months, the embryo is called a **fetus** (FEE-tuhs).

The specific connection between the embryo and the mother is the **umbilical** (umh-BILL-uh-kulh) cord that forms to link the embryo to the **placenta** (pluh-SEN-tuh). Food and oxygen are received directly from the mother's bloodstream to the placenta, and then through the umbilical cord to the embryo. The elimination of waste takes place in the same way.

Because of this direct linkage between mother and fetus, the pregnant mother-to-be should eat nutritionally and avoid all drugs unless they are prescribed by her doctor—including alcohol, tobacco, caffeine, and over-the-counter medications. Whatever the mother takes into her body, she shares with her growing child. Remember that

Fetal Development

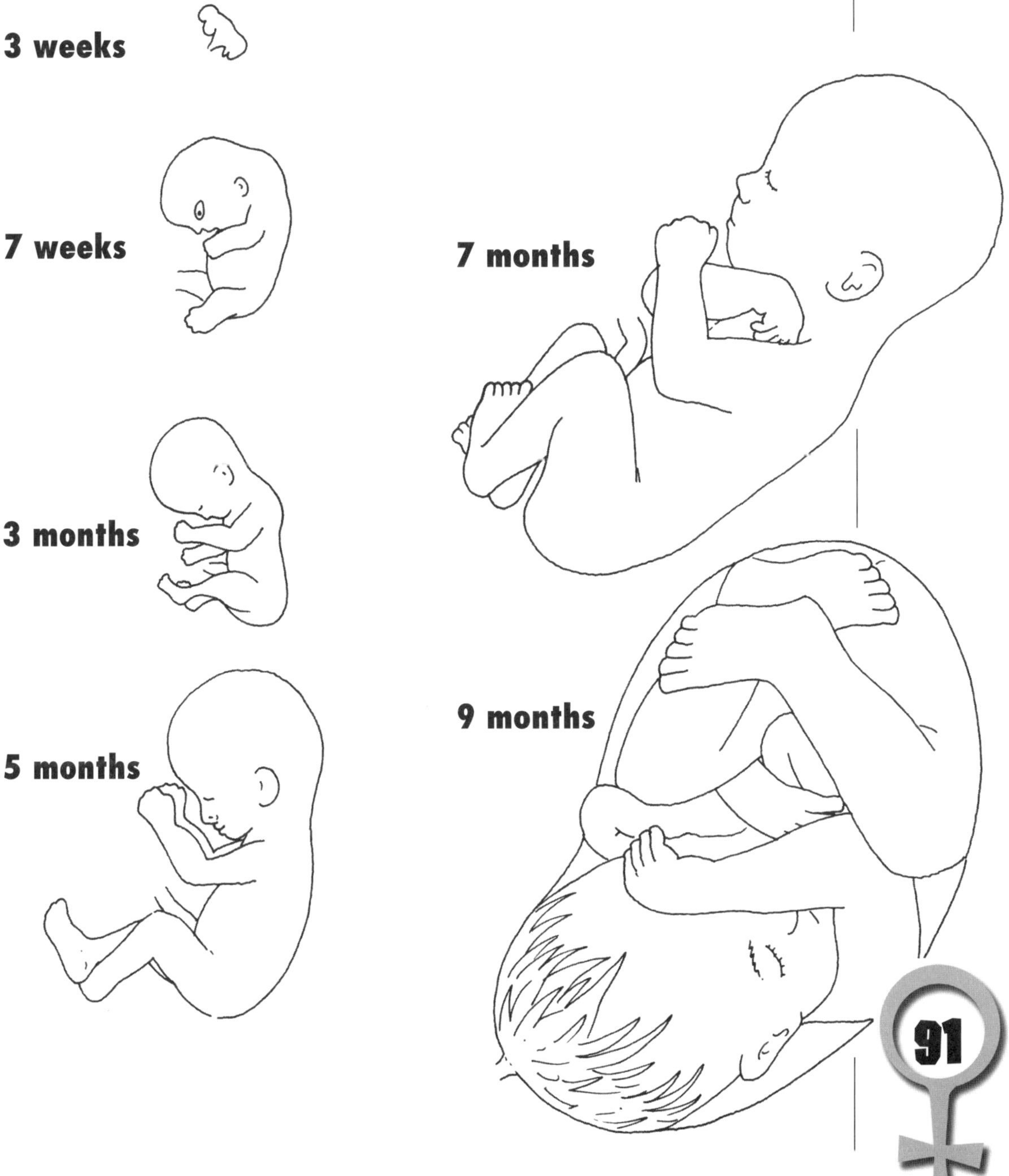

3 weeks 

7 weeks 

3 months 

5 months 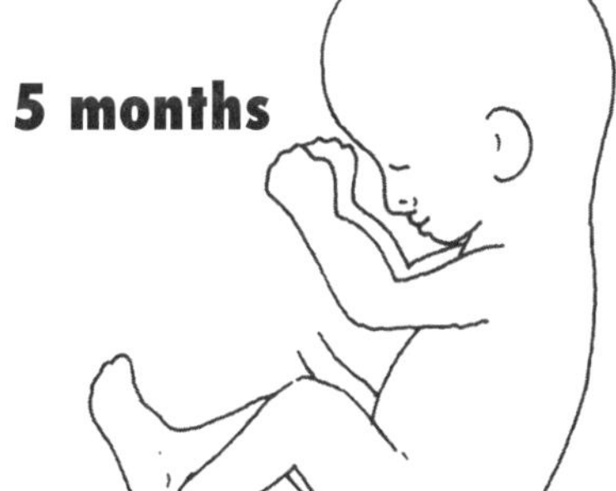

7 months

9 months

91

our bodies are made up of chemicals, and the growth of the embryo/fetus is a series of chemical reactions.

During pregnancy, the baby is surrounded and protected by the **amnion** (AM-nee-uhn) or **amniotic** (am-nee-Ah-tik) **sac.** The baby is suspended in a watery fluid inside the sac.

A Time to Be Born

An average pregnancy lasts nine months or 40 weeks. When it's time for the birth, the pituitary gland secretes a hormone that causes the muscles of the uterus to **contract** (kuhn-TRACT) or shorten. These **contractions** (kuhn-TRACK-shuns) are mild and far apart as the mother's body moves the baby into position for birth. We call that action, along with the contractions, **labor.**

As labor continues, the contractions become stronger, more frequent, and last longer. The muscles push the baby downward toward the cervix—the lower end of the uterus. The increasing pressure of the baby against the cervix causes the cervix to **dilate** (DIE-late) or open up.

At some point during labor the amniotic sac breaks, and the woman feels a gush of fluid as it flows from the uterus and out of the vagina. If you have heard people talk about an expectant mother whose "water broke," this is what they were talking about. Once the cervix has opened enough for the baby to pass through, the baby, usually head first, is pushed through the vagina and out of the body—the step called **delivery.**

Giving birth is hard work for the mother, which explains why the time it takes to position a baby for birth is called labor. It is a time of considerable pain and discomfort, although there are medications available to lessen that pain. Many couples spend the last several weeks of pregnancy attending child-birth training classes. In these classes the couple is instructed in proper breathing techniques, how to focus attention on something other than the pain, and how the father can coach the mother during labor and delivery. Simply knowing what is

happening can reduce worries and discomfort. Sharing in this experience together strengthens the father's bond to the new baby and often increases his appreciation of and love for his wife.

Once the baby is born, the umbilical cord is cut and clamped or tied, separating the baby from the mother. Since the umbilical cord doesn't contain nerve tissue, there is no pain. The stump of that umbilical cord remains on the baby, and within 10 days will dry up and fall off. What remains is what we often call the belly button or **navel** (NAY-vuhl). The contractions continue until they push the placenta out of the uterus. For several weeks following the delivery, bleeding may continue as the mother's body rids itself of tissue that was required during pregnancy but is no longer needed.

Sometimes another way

When the baby is coming out anything but head first, it is called a **breech** birth and may require a surgical delivery—also called a **caesarean section** (sih-ZARE-ee-uhn) or C-section. (Julius Caesar is believed to have been delivered surgically, which is how this procedure came to be known as a caesarean section.) If the doctor can't manipulate the mother's abdomen and get the baby turned, an incision is made through the abdomen and into the uterus. The doctor removes the baby and then stitches the incision. There are other reasons for doing a surgical delivery, for example a sudden drop in the baby's heart rate, or the baby's head is too large for the mother's pelvis (the bones that surround her vagina), or concerns about either mother or child. Unless there are complications, babies born by caesarean section are as healthy as those delivered vaginally; mothers giving birth this way may need longer to recover.

Stages of Childbirth

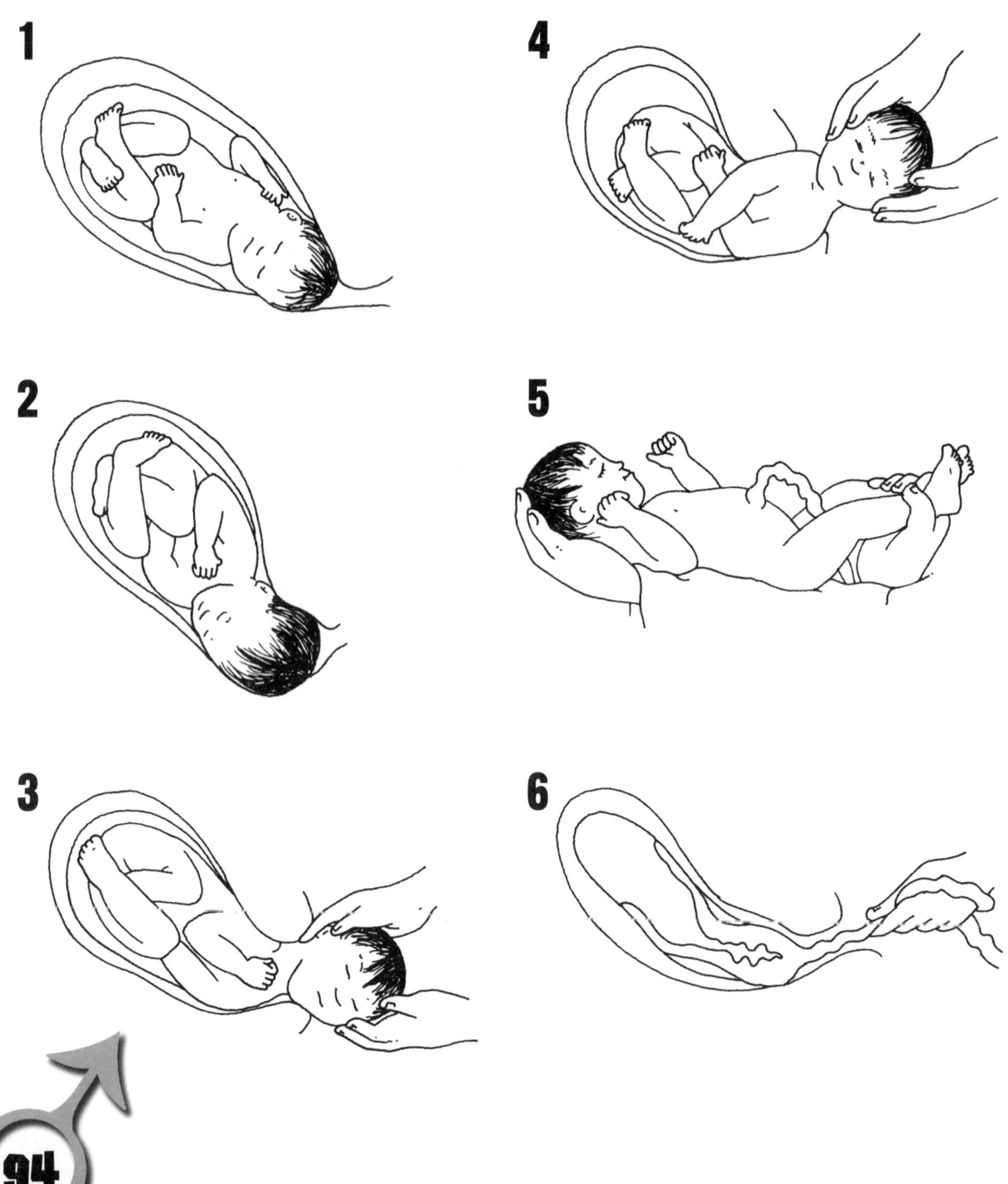

Boys and girls generally have lots and lots of questions about multiple births (twins, triplets, or more). But basically, the question is "How do they happen?" There are two ways:

<u>More than one ovum, more than one sperm</u>: Instead of releasing just one ovum each month, sometimes the ovaries release more. If each of the ova is fertilized (each by a different sperm), leading to the development of two or more embryos, they become what we call **fraternal** or non-identical, related like all brothers and sisters, only sharing the same birthday. Since each ovum was fertilized by a different sperm, they may or may not be the same sex and may or may not look alike.

<u>One ovum, one sperm</u>: Remember how the cells begin to divide following conception? Sometimes this cluster of cells splits into two separate clusters. And because each cluster has **identical** genetic information, the two babies must be the same gender, and will have a majority of characteristics in common. If one or more of the cell clusters split again, you could have identical triplets or quadruplets. It's very unlikely that it would go further than this.

<u>Siamese (or conjoined) twins?</u> Identical twins whose cells did not fully divide early in their development are known as conjoined twins. Two babies develop, but they may be connected in a wide variety of ways: heart, brain, liver, and so forth. Every situation is different, and some babies can be successfully separated, while some can't. This happens rarely but when it does, the news reports make us think it is more common than what it really is.

Quintuplets? Octuplets? Within the last few years, octuplets and other large groups of children have been born at once. How does this happen? With advanced medical technology, doctors are able to give medications to women who are not able to naturally produce ova, allowing couples to have children. However, sometimes the medication causes too many ova, and all of them become fertilized either during sexual intercourse or during laboratory fertilization, called "invitro fertilization" or IVF. This can be both a blessing and a challenge for the struggling parents.

Your birth, and the birth of every living creature, is a miracle. Our understanding of a miracle is something that seems impossible but happens anyway. That's a miracle and that is you! Think about it. The combination of any sperm and ova make for a different person every time. If there were only 100 sperm and 100 ova, there would be 10,000 possible combinations. But there are billions of sperm produced by the testicles every month, and hundreds of thousands of ova in female ovaries. Imagine the possibilities!

You are the product of one particular ovum and one particular sperm. So the simple fact that you are, and that you are who you are, makes you a miracle—God's miracle.

> When I look at your heavens,
>   the work of your fingers,
> the moon and the stars that you have established;
> what are human beings that you are mindful of them,
>   mortals that you care for them?
> Yet you have made them a little lower than God,
>   and crowned them with glory and honor.
>
> (Psalm 8:3-5)

Chapter 6

The Question Box

Things kids want to know
Things kids need to know

Opening the Question Box: Questions Kids Have Asked

Adolescence + Freedom = Responsibility

"Cutting the cord" is a phrase people often use to describe this move toward independence, referring to the **umbilical cord** (uhm-BILL-uh-kuhl), which connected you to your mother and supplied you with nourishment and oxygen as you grew and developed before you were born.

Now is the time to "cut the cord" further as you begin to establish yourself as an adolescent and to claim the new freedom it brings. With that freedom comes more opportunities to be on your own and make your own decisions. Decision-making calls for responsibility.

We want you to have correct information so you can make wise decisions about your behavior and your treatment of others. Your response then is your Christian witness and can affect your health and well-being and the health and well-being of others. We will talk about concerns that confuse and even frighten young persons—concerns that are regularly in the Question Box at sessions of *Created by God*.

<blockquote>
Finally, beloved, whatever is true, whatever is honorable, whatever is just, whatever is pure, whatever is pleasing, whatever is commendable, if there is any excellence and if there is anything worthy of praise, think about these things.

(Philippians 4:8)
</blockquote>

When the apostle Paul wrote to new Christians in Philippi, he knew they were dealing with questions about how to live and what to believe. He wisely advised them to make room for positive thoughts such as truth, honor, justice, and excellence. That means clearing out the negative—confusion, ignorance, and worry. So, let's get clearing!

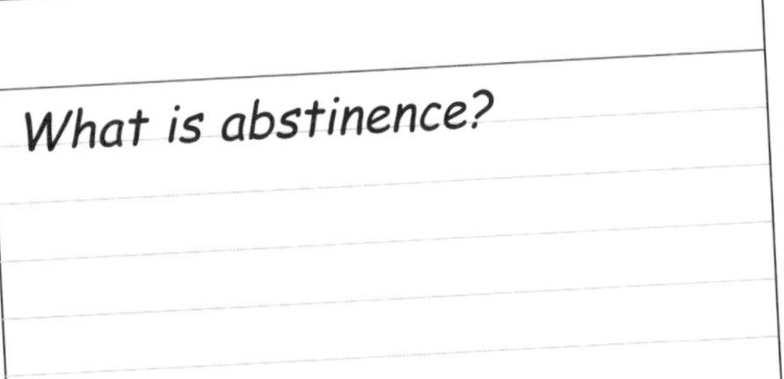 Abstinence

Abstinence (AB-stuh-nuhns) is not having sexual intercourse between now and when you are married. Your family and your church strongly urges you to make that decision, even while they recognize that you are becoming physically capable of sexual intercourse, and that you now experience sexual arousal or excitement. Sexual intercourse is for married adults.

Abstinence allows for relational intimacy to develop and maturity to occur. (Look back at Chapter 4.)

Young persons who have sexual intercourse end up missing out on all of the talking that leads to intimacy. Guilt and embarrassment prevent them from talking with each other about sex or anything else. Sexual intercourse is a good gift, but when this good gift is used unwisely, it can destroy intimacy.

As Paul writes to the people of the Corinthian church, "Love is patient" (1 Corinthians 13:4a). Being patient when it comes to sexual intercourse is an act of kindness—toward yourself, toward that person for whom you have special feelings, and toward the many other people who stand to be affected if you make the decision to have sexual relations while you are young.

Setting yourself up to feel guilty is foolish. Not thinking of the many people who will be affected by your actions is selfish. It is not unusual for young persons to have little upon which to build a lasting relationship, but they feel forced to stay together because they have had or are having intercourse.

Love is patient. 1 Corinthians 13:4a

Here are some other reasons for abstinence:

- Contracting one or more sexually transmitted diseases (see page 132).
- Uncommitted sex means one is taking advantage of the other.
- You will miss the intimate relationship God intends for us with our life partner.
- Pregnancy can happen. Are you prepared—emotionally and financially—to be a parent now?
- The younger the mother, the greater possibility of pregnancy and delivery complications.
- Your life dreams and plans will be drastically changed.

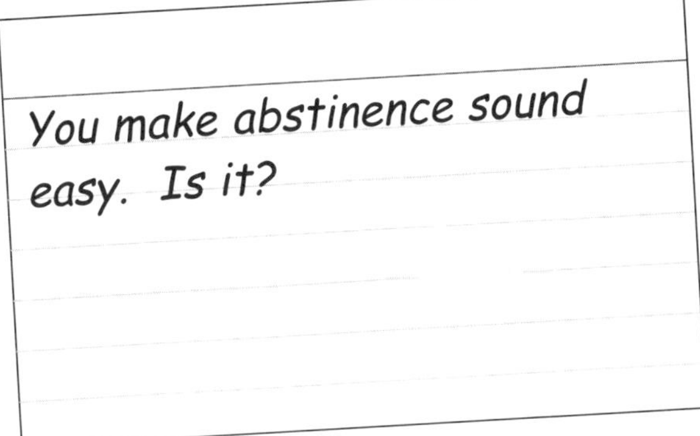

Oh no. You will find someone you're attracted to, think you're in love with, and you may forget all these reasons. DON'T. You may hear the argument, "But I love you." That is still not enough reason if you are not ready—emotionally, relationally, academically, financially—to make the commitment of marriage. Here are some ways to maintain abstinence:

- Prayerfully decide to abstain. Then keep praying about it.
- Tell a trusted friend or mentor about your decision; ask that person to pray for you.
- Don't believe the rumors about how everyone is "doing it." Many aren't.
- Stand for what is right for you.
- Concentrate on building intimate friendships.
- Plan ahead: avoid situations where you will be tempted.

<table>
<tr><td>

What is abuse?

</td></tr>
</table>

Abuse literally means "improper use." There are many kinds of abuse: verbal (language), bullying, disrespect. Think of it this way: Any action that treats part of God's creation with disrespect is abuse. Whenever God's good gift of sexuality is being misused, you can be sure that abuse is taking place. Specifically, **sexual abuse** is any kind of touching of the body that causes sexual stimulation, especially of the genital areas that is unwanted or inappropriate. Sexual abuse may or may not include intercourse. In other words, if you are touched in a way that makes you uncomfortable, that is sexual abuse.

Molestation (MAH-lehs-TAY-shun), the sexual abuse of children, does happen: approximately 30% of girls and 17% of boys are sexually abused before turning 18. Who are abusers? Sometimes they are strangers, but more often the abuser is someone the young person knows and trusts—a relative, a neighbor, a teacher, a pastor, or a coach. Most sex abusers are men, but women can be abusive as well. You don't have to worry every minute about being abused, but it's smart to be cautious. Avoid being alone in places where it would be difficult to get help if you needed it. Understand your body and your sexuality. This understanding will help you to be aware of potential abuse and to do something about it. Lastly, listen to your body. It will tell you that it's afraid before your mouth is able to say so. Trust your feelings.

Persons guilty of sexually abusing children:

- **act** intentionally. It happens on purpose.
- **misuse power or trust.** Kids want attention and love. An abuser wants sexual contact.
- **take advantage of vulnerability.** Abusers target kids who are vulnerable emotionally, socially, relationally.
- **offer alcohol or drugs.**
- **insist on secrecy.** Abusers tell children to keep the secret.
- **make impossible promises.** I will love you forever. This is an attempt to make you feel more like an adult.
- **sometimes sexually abuse members of their own family.** This is called **incest** (IN-sest).
- **threaten.** If you tell anyone, I'll blame you, or I'll hurt your family. Or, in cases of incest, they threaten that reporting the abuse will break up the family.
- **abuse more than one time and more than one child.** The abuser will continue until stopped.
- **are not emotionally or mentally healthy persons.** They only care about themselves.
- **start with seemingly innocent actions.** A little touching can lead to more overt sexual behaviors.
- **are always wrong.** Always. No exceptions. Any sexual contact between an adult and a child (defined as under 18) is wrong, against the law, and always the fault of the older person.
- **must always be reported.** Again, no exceptions. It won't just go away. Help is needed.

This is not a problem that persons—whether they are the abusers or the abused—can handle alone.

Again, sexual abuse in any form is always wrong, and is never the fault of the victim. If you or some one you know is victimized, tell someone immediately. If that person doesn't respond, tell someone else until someone does listen. Know that teachers, pastors, and doctors are required by law to report abuse.

> My baby sitter touched me once. What should I do?

"Touched" you? What exactly do you mean? Now that you have read this book, you understand more about human bodies and inappropriate sexual touch. If that is what happened, then you need to talk with your parent or a trusted adult, immediately.

> What is "rape"? What is "date rape"?

Rape is forced sexual intercourse. It is abuse and can be committed by a complete stranger or by someone the victim has been very close to—even sexually active with in the past. It makes no difference—what matters is the setting now. When one person forces an unwilling person to have sex, that is rape. When this happens on a date, it is called date rape. Guys have no right to expect sex or to insist on sex simply because they have taken a girl out, no matter how many times they have

been out together or how long they have been dating. Even when a couple is married, forced sexual intercourse is rape. No means no. Remember this rule: When it comes to sex, the one who says "No" is always the one who is right.

> **What is a prostitute?**

A **prostitute** (PROSS-tuh-toot) is a person paid to perform sexual acts. Prostitutes are frequently the victims of violence and put themselves at risk for diseases spread by sexual contact. Prostitution is illegal in most places.

Birth Control and Responsible Family Planning

> **Why do people have sex when they don't want to have children?**

"Sex" (or sexual intercourse) is not just about having children. It is the wonderful experience of sharing love together. Married couples enjoy sex—even when they do not want to become pregnant. When sexually active couples want to avoid pregnancy, they must decide in advance how that will happen. Taking chances with possible pregnancy is a BAD idea. The average pregnancy rate for couples using no form of birth control is 85%. The couple must—together—decide about a method of birth control, which is any method used to prevent pregnancy.

Abstinence, which we've already discussed, means not having (or abstaining from) **intercourse**. *Not having sexual intercourse is the only absolute guarantee that pregnancy will not happen. For unmarried persons, it is the wisest and most Godly choice.*

> ## How does birth control work?

There are several forms.

Natural Family Planning uses timed abstinence. The couple must carefully watch for signs of ovulation—such as the woman's body temperature—and avoid sexual intercourse on days when conception is possible. But pregnancy still results about 27% of the time.

Birth control pills require a doctor's prescription. They provide hormones similar to those produced naturally when the woman is pregnant, which prevent her ovaries from releasing ova. But pregnancy still results about 8% of the time.

Hormones can also be administered by *injection* every three months. The advantage is not having to take a pill daily. Pregnancy still results 3% of the time.

Patches can be placed on the skin every week that also deliver the hormones into a woman's system. Like pills, the average pregnancy rate for this methods is 8%.

Intrauterine device (in-tra-YOO-truh-in) or **IUD** is either a soft plastic or metal ring, coil, or loop that is inserted and removed from the uterus by a doctor. It contains hormones that are released for up to five years. Pregnancy results less than 1% of the time.

Plastic rods or *implants* may be inserted in the arm under the skin to deliver hormones for up to five years. The average pregnancy rate is similar to the IUD.

A **diaphragm** (DIE-uh-fram) is a flexible latex dome-shaped cup that is inserted into the vagina by the woman before having sexual intercourse. Prescribed by a doctor, the diaphragm is positioned over the cervix and blocks sperm from entering the uterus. Should any sperm get around the barrier, spermicidal foam (see below) immobilizes them.

A **cervical cap** is smaller and fits securely over and seals off the cervix. Both the diaphragm and the cervical cap are reusable. Pregnancy still results 16% of the time.

Spermicidal foam, cream, jelly, film, or suppositories can each be used alone and do not require a prescription. Pregnancy still results about 29% of the time for each.

A **condom** (KON-duhm) is a thin rubber or latex sheath for the penis that looks like a long, rolled-up, oversized balloon. It is placed on the erect penis before sexual intercourse to prevent the spread of sexually transmitted disease and/or to prevent pregnancy. When used properly, it captures the semen and prevents sperm from getting inside the woman's body. Pregnancy still results about 21% of the time.

Couples who decide not to have children or not to have any more children may choose sterilization, which is the surgical procedure to make a person permanently incapable of reproduction. A woman might have a **tubal ligation** (TOO-buhl lie-GAY-shun) where her fallopian tubes are cut, tied, or sealed to prevent pregnancy. A man might have a **vasectomy** (vah-SEHK-tuh-me), which cuts the vas deferens, preventing sperm from mixing with the semen and exiting the body. The ovaries continue to release ova, and the testicles continue to produce sperm, but both ova and sperm are absorbed by the body.

Yes, persons who have had these surgeries can continue to have sex. Men continue to ejaculate semen, but it does not contain sperm.

There is disagreement about **contraception** (KON-truh-SEHP-shuhn) and sin. However, most faith traditions and individuals agree that responsible parenting—having only wanted and intentional children—is the most faithful choice, honoring the life that God gives us.

> **Why are boys so weird?**

> **Why are girls so weird?**

Lots of kids your age are still in the "girls are weird/boys are weird" phase. The "weirdness" boys see in girls and girls see in boys is really recognition of the basic differences, not just how they look but how they think, perceive, and respond, without appreciating them. But that's the charm of relationships! And the solution is respect, information, and time spent together.

Someone once asked, "I'm not really interested in the other sex yet. Is there something wrong with me?" Nope, nothing wrong. You're just not interested. No big deal. Kids entering adolescence are all over the map in terms of social development, just as they are with physical development.

> **When is it OK to date and what do people do on a date?**

First of all, not all the people your age are dating, although some are. And the definition of "dating" or "going out" varies. Parents give permission for different kinds of dating at different ages. And teens show interest in dating at different ages. So, "normal" here is variation. Whether you are or aren't dating, it's natural to be wondering why people date and what happens when they do.

111

Dating is one way for two people to get to know each other. It's like any other act of friendship: you talk, laugh, share experiences, and go places together. Friendships generally start with what people have in common: living near each other, liking the same kind of music, playing on the same team, sitting beside each other in class, going to the same church, playing in the band, to name a few possibilities. Although same-gender friends share these commonalities too, with males and females a special attraction can develop. People are drawn together not just because they are alike in many ways, but also because they are different. The differences give them lots to talk and learn about. For starters, consider group dating. Think of it like swimming. Have a buddy—or even lots of buddies! Group dating makes the most sense at first—perhaps for quite a while. More people means more people to talk with. More people means less attention focused on you and less pressure to "perform." Group dating allows people to relax and be themselves. Group dating can also be helpful when we are tempted toward inappropriate sexual activity.

Dating allows us to practice our social skills and to get better at relating to others. Dating doesn't have to be about finding your future spouse, but it can help us begin to know what qualities we enjoy in someone we are getting closer to—and what ones we don't enjoy.

Dating can present problems when respect for self and others isn't given a high priority. Be smart. Understand yourself, your feelings, and the way your mind and body react when you are close to another person, holding hands, hugging, and kissing. Talking together about these matters shows your care and respect for each other. Make decisions NOW about how much physical and sexual touching is too much FOR YOU. (See the section about Abstinence.)

Perhaps you've recognized special feelings for a particular person and wonder if it's love. Maybe you're wondering about the future: how will I know the "right one" for me? You've known people who claim to be in love and wonder how they knew. And you most likely know some who once were in love but aren't anymore. You wonder, Were they really in love? Were they mistaken? Did they fall out of love? The lives of many girls and boys have been touched directly by the divorce of parents or indirectly by the divorce of other family members, neighbors, or friends' parents. Are there ways to avoid making mistakes?

We start by realizing that we were created by God to love many people, not just one. There are many people who are possible lifelong partners for us, not just one. You will be meeting lots of people in the next several years. You will be developing friendships with many of those people. With some of those friends you will work at building intimacy. Perhaps there will be one special person you will decide to marry—one person to whom you will commit your life. Regardless of how a special relationship begins, it requires work to get stronger and to last. We think that our bodies will provide very specific signals when *like* turns to *love*. But our physical attraction isn't the only criteria for a marriage partner or even for a person to date. We need to use our minds to discover those who are attractive to us in other ways with questions, such as

- Who do I enjoy being with more than anyone else?
- Who makes me feel good about myself?
- Who do I always enjoy discovering new things about?
- Who values what I consider to be important?
- Who wants to be close to me but doesn't insist that we do everything together?
- Who do I trust with my personal thoughts and feelings?

Although you're far from ready to get married, think about these words from a marriage service that many pastors use:

**God the Eternal keep you in love with each other,
so that the peace of Christ may abide in your home.
Go to serve God and your neighbor in all that you do.**

Then the pastor says to everyone:

**Bear witness to the love of God in this world,
so that those to whom love is a stranger
will find in you generous friends.***

What you feel for and experience with one person sometimes brings out the very best in you and helps you to be more loving toward others. That is a good sign that you are in love.

* From "A Service of Christian Marriage" in *The United Methodist Hymnal;* © 1989 The United Methodist Publishing House; p. 869. Reprinted by permission.

Heterosexual, Homosexual and Sexual Orientation

> ### What is a homosexual?

Sexual orientation (or-ee-ehn-TAY-shun) is the "direction" of a person's sexual attractions or feelings. *Hetero* means different, so **heterosexual** (HEHT-uh-roh-SEHK-shoo-uhl) means sexual feelings for the other gender (male toward female and vice versa). *Homo* means the same, so **homosexual** (HOH-moh-SEHK-shoo-uhl) means sexual feelings for one's own gender (male toward male, female toward female). The term **gay** was first applied just to male homosexuals, but is used today to refer to either males or females. **Lesbian** (LEZ-bee-uhn) is another term for a female homosexual. **Bisexual** (bie-SEKS-yoo-uhl) refers to sexual feelings for both genders.

These three sexual orientations appear to be very clear. In reality, however, people are very complex. This complexity is reflected in who they find themselves sexually attracted to. Each individual is different.

> ### Why are some people gay?

Put simply, no one knows. Lots of research continues to be done by people who study brains, genes, hormones, personalities, cultures, and the Bible, but they do not yet agree on a reason. Sexual orientation could be determined by the combination of chromosomes and genes that makes us who we are. Or, as some

believe, our sexual orientation might be shaped by our relationships and experiences—both the good and the bad, and that one can choose his or her sexual orientation. Most likely, many factors determine to whom one is attracted. So the answer to the question? We do not know.

Observing a person's interests, behaviors, personality, clothing, or body type cannot tell us for sure what that person's sexual orientation might be. Some people fit cultural stereotypes for femininity or masculinity, and some don't. Remember that one's sexual orientation is only one factor in what makes a person who he or she is.

We need to relate to people based on what we do know: all of us are created by God and loved by God. As God's children, we must never hurt others by taking advantage of them because of their sexuality, real or perceived. Remember Jesus' story of the Good Samaritan and his conclusion that we are called to love our neighbors, often those who are different from ourselves, as we love ourselves (Luke 10:25-37).

A person is "gay" or "homosexual" if he or she directs his or her sexual desire toward a person of the same gender on an ongoing basis. You may at times have sexual feelings for your classmates of either gender. This can be confusing. This does not mean you're a homosexual. Remember that adolescence is a time of growing and developing, of many physical surges and new social relationships. With your body experiencing new feelings and stimulation, it may react at times you do not expect. And, in today's world, the media can lead us to think that a large percentage of persons are homosexual. That is not true.

Having said all that, it is not necessary to declare one's sexuality while you are in the "discovery phase" of adolescence. Just as you don't

have to declare your life's work, your husband or wife, or your college major now, you don't need to decide about your sexual orientation. Enjoy your life, wait and see. Remember that God is with you, loving you throughout the discovery. Again, do not draw any conclusions about your sexuality. There is no specific and exact timetable and pattern for adolescence.

Intercourse

> Does it hurt to have sexual intercourse?

Generally, no. We say generally, with some explanations. The first is this: Since the vagina of a female who has not had sexual intercourse has not been stretched, she may experience some discomfort at the beginning. The second is, if she is fearful, her muscles will tighten around her vagina, making entry by the penis painful. And third, because women respond more gradually to stimulation, her natural lubrication may not be sufficient when intercourse is attempted.

> When are people finished being sexual?

Never. Being sexual is part of what it means to be human—from the moment of conception and throughout all of life. We continue to be either male or female, and relate to others as such, even after persons don't fit the stereotypes for "sexy." To be created in the image of God is to be created male or female. All persons are sexual always.

117

The Internet and Chat Rooms

> **What's wrong with what I can watch on the Internet?**

Although the Internet brings us much that is good, it also is a door to much that is bad for all of us—children, tweens, teens, and adults. Unlike most other media, there is no regulation. Persons can put *anything* on the Internet. And, we are often curious about whatever is not healthy for us, including violence and sexual perversions. If we watch or read something frequently, we start believing it's normal. We forget the standards of our faith and our family. It can be like secondhand smoke: we think it's not affecting us, but it really is making us sick on the inside. (See the paragraphs about pornography, pages 126–127.)

A chat room is a public forum: Anything you say could be repeated to millions of people in a matter of moments. Next, people aren't always who they say they are. Some people make up new identities and then play

> **What are the dangers of a chat room?**

them out in places like chat rooms. And, some people use this technology to set up abusive encounters. The danger comes when a young person gives away personal information that can tell an abuser where he or she lives, or when that young person believes the fictitious identity.

You can't really know. But you can keep yourself safe by taking certain precautions. Limit your chat room conversations to persons you already know. Don't "meet" new persons there. Never give out personal information—anything that would enable someone to find you—like your last name, telephone number, mailing address, parent's names, or school and team names.

If you ignore all of the above, do not make arrangements to meet anyone face to face that you have met on the Internet, especially without your parents' knowledge.

To "cyber" or have "cybersex" is to use instant messaging or chat rooms to talk about sex or show nude photos of oneself with the intent of sexually arousing someone long distance. (See the information about pornography and sexting on pages 126 and 131.)

Blog stands for "web log" and is basically a public online diary—that is public and permanent, available to anyone and forever. Some people use blogs to record sexual thoughts or sexual experiences. Be very careful: what you write today could be read, years later, by a prospective employer and could cost you a job. A good rule of thumb: If you wouldn't want your parent or grandparent to read it, don't put it in a blog.

Those who say, "I love God," and hate their brothers or sisters, are liars; for those who do not love a brother or sister whom they have seen, cannot love God whom they have not seen. The commandment we have from God is this: those who love God must love their brothers and sisters also. (1 John 4:20-21, adapted)

We want you to know all about your bodies, how they work, and what a wonderful gift God has given you. We want you to be able to talk about your body to doctors and anyone necessary, using the right terms. And we want you to be able to honor God and yourself by speaking about the human body with respect.

In *Created By God* sessions, we review some of the slang terms used in reference to bodies and behaviors. Most of them are not acceptable in conversation and are considered "bad" or "dirty" or as swear words. We are not encouraging you to use them, but we know that you need to know what they mean, and the best way is to relate them to the more technical words you have learned in this study.

You may know persons who are only able to joke about sexuality, where they have an audience. We're guessing they don't know what all the words even mean, and likely don't know the correct words. We encourage you to know and use the correct words when appropriate, both to honor God and to communicate clearly.

Why do you teach scientific words for our bodies instead of the words we hear from our friends?

Why do people talk about sex on the school bus?

Why do people use swear words at school?

Do they think it makes them look cool or tough?

Words are more than collections of letters or sounds. Words can be used to make persons feel good or bad about themselves and about their world. Offensive language assaults another person—it intimidates, embarrasses, and triggers anger. <u>People use slang words or offensive language to get attention.</u> When offensive language related to bodies or sexuality is used, it suggests that sex itself—which is God's good creation—is offensive and dirty. When we understand and think positively about our sexuality, putting people down by calling them slang terms for our genitals just doesn't make sense.

How creative is the human mind? There are an unlimited number of slang terms, and new ones are created every day. But most are words and phrases that have been used for many, many years.

And as far as offensive words "slipping out on accident," if they weren't in our heads and in our vocabularies in the first place, they wouldn't be there to slip out. And we make decisions daily about what to listen to and what we read or view. When we

react to something without thinking, we rely on the words that we use or hear most often. The more we use offensive words, the more we will come to rely on them, and the more easily they will "slip out." So, as a Christian, don't listen to those words, and don't use them.

Practice the proper terms until you become comfortable with them. The best words are the ones that communicate most clearly to the most people—the words that celebrate God's great gift of sexuality and inform and build people up.

Masturbation

Masturbation is touching or rubbing one's own genitals in a way that produces strong, pleasant, sexual feelings. "Weird" would mean that it is something out of the ordinary, which it isn't. Most people masturbate at some point in their lives—some for their whole lives. Because of the rush of hormones during adolescence, this is a time when many people masturbate. It's certainly true that some don't, and that is perfectly OK as well.

Have you observed babies as they discover their hands and then their feet? They also discover their genitals and find that touching them feels good. During puberty, young people sort of "rediscover" their genitals because penises and vulvas respond to touch with very intense sensations. Masturbation is a private and safe way to experience these feelings. It does not involve "using" another person for personal pleasure, cannot lead to pregnancy, and does not put a person at risk for a sexually transmitted disease.

Masturbation may bring strong negative reactions from adults, some of whom were taught that masturbation is wrong and possibly harmful. It is neither, but even actions that are not wrong or harmful can still create problems. We emphasize that masturbation is not a substitute for relationships. We caution that, although rough handling of the genitals will not cause permanent damage, it may cause soreness and irritation. And it does not lessen one's ability to enjoy sexual relations as an adult.

According to the Bible, Jesus has nothing to say about masturbation. But if it interferes with your relationship with God—meaning you feel embarrassed or guilty—or with others, then perhaps you are preoccupied with masturbation.

> What is oral sex?

> Why do people want to have oral sex?

> Is it a sin?

Sex, besides intercourse, is activity that stimulates a person sexually. Oral refers to the mouth, so you put the two words together and get sex that involves mouths—specifically, mouths and genitals. It's at this point that most kids go, "Oh yuck!" or "Gross!" We discuss it here because we read the reports that many tweens and teens have questions or are experimenting with this behavior.

Oral sex is sexual activity where genitals and mouths touch. Why would people want to do that? Genitals are very sensitive. They respond to touch. Mouths are also very sensitive (which is why people kiss). Put two sensitive body parts together, and the resulting feelings are very strong. Yes, oral sex is sometimes experienced by adults within marriage. When people have committed their lives to one another, each is set free to enjoy the body of the other. If they both agree to it, it is okay.

But here we're talking about young persons and it's not okay. Oral sex is about sexual feelings, not about intimacy, love, and commitment. For guys looking for the sensation of oral sex, it's not an act of caring and respect but just the opposite. The guy who convinces someone to perform oral sex on him will likely feel a great sense of accomplishment and power because he got what he wanted. The person who performs oral sex will likely feel used and powerless.

Definitely. That's why it's sometimes called "oral intercourse." Some kids participate in oral sex as an alternative to vaginal sex, rationalizing that they can remain (technically) virgins and can't get pregnant. (Which is true.) Oral sex is a very intimate activity: it's really sex.

Is oral sex really sex?

Is oral sex dangerous?

Can you get STDs from oral sex?

Could you get pregnant from doing it?

Can it lead to pregnancy? No. *Can it be responsible for the spread of sexually transmitted diseases?* It can and it is. Among young people, oral sex is the leading cause for the increase in sexually transmitted diseases. We'd say that's pretty dangerous!

124

> **What is peer pressure?**

Your peers are persons with whom you associate. Pressure is applying force to make something happen. Put them together and you get peer pressure, which can be both positive and negative. Sometimes peer pressure encourages us toward a positive experience. But more often peer pressure is negative—being talked in to doing something we shouldn't or don't want to do. Sometimes that negative act is sexual activity.

A. You want to be ACCEPTED.

B. You BELIEVE that "everyone is doing it" (they're not).

C. Your hormone-active body is STIMULATED.

> **How does peer pressure work?**

Jesus had peer pressure too. His disciples tried to pressure him into sending the crowds away to find food, but Jesus responded by feeding them with five loaves of bread and two small fish. As he entered Jerusalem for the last time on Palm Sunday, the crowds were pressuring Jesus to be the kind of Messiah or Savior they wanted him to be—one who would overthrow the Romans. And because Jesus was human as well as divine, he probably had physical temptations as well. Standing up to these temptations, Jesus showed that he had more power—the power that came from God, and from knowing who he was and what he was called to do.

You are a child of God, created for an intimate relationship with God and for a special intimate relationship with another person. Knowing that, you have power over all peer pressure that you might experience.

125

Phone Sex

> What is phone sex?

"Phone sex" is talk that stimulates one or both of the persons to sexual arousal, and often to orgasm. Phone sex is not about a loving relationship but about physical gratification. Because we believe that our sexuality is a gift from God for relationship and sometimes for procreation (making a new life), we also believe that phone sex distorts God's gift. (Also see Sexting, page 131.)

Pornography

> What is pornography?

> Is it wrong to look at pictures of naked people?

Pornography (pore-NAGH-ruh-fee) is sexually explicit media—photos, art, movies, books, or conversations. What does explicit mean? Nothing is left to the imagination. Pornography abuses or improperly uses God's good gift of sexuality. But it's more than nudity.

What is the difference between great art like Michelangelo's nude statue of King David and a picture from a pornographic magazine or website? It's this: Michelangelo intended to depict the beauty of God's human creations and cause us to go "Ah!" while the other is intended to excite us sexually and cause us to go "Woo-woo!" One treats a

person as a person and the other treats a person as an object or thing. Through pornography, women are treated as objects. Men are treated as objects. Children are treated as objects. Violence paired with sex and rape is approved. Sex between adults and children is promoted. This is what pornography is about.

Pornography is addictive—just like alcohol, tobacco, and many other drugs. A little makes some people want more and more. Easy Internet access makes it easy to feed that addiction. Instead of affirming the beauty of the human body and the goodness of God's gift of sexuality, pornographers (the persons who produce and sell pornographic material) take advantage of human curiosity and turn it into a money-making enterprise.

After prolonged exposure to pornography, some persons not only begin to believe that the behaviors and attitudes they see there are acceptable, but they also begin to act them out. Police reports document that pornography is linked to acts of sexual violence. The only way to deal with an addiction is to avoid that which is addictive.

How does a woman know when she is pregnant?

Once pregnancy has occurred, the menstrual periods stop, so not having a period is a first sign. Other factors—involvement in athletics, poor health, and emotional stress, for example—can affect regularity of the menstrual cycle, so other special tests must be done by a doctor to make sure. Some women experience what is often called **morning sickness.** Particularly during the first three months, women may experience nausea and/or vomiting, usually but not always in the morning.

Are there other bodily changes?

Yes there are, but not all women experience all of them. First, the breasts become sensitive to the touch and enlarge, preparing to produce milk for the mother to breast-feed her baby if she chooses. The abdomen enlarges to accommodate the baby growing inside. As the uterus grows, it presses on the bladder, causing pregnant women to need to urinate more often. Some women experience cravings for certain foods, which can be the body's way of asking for certain types of nourishment.

Yes, they can continue to have intercourse. The amniotic sac and fluid keep the fetus well-protected in the uterus. Unless there is a problem with the pregnancy, most couples can continue having sexual intercourse until close to the time of birth—or until it becomes uncomfortable. It won't hurt the fetus.

Sometimes a pregnant woman's body recognizes that there are serious problems with the embryo or fetus and automatically ends the pregnancy. We call this a **miscarriage** (MISS-kare-ihj) or **spontaneous abortion** (spahn-TAY-nee-uhs ah-BORE-shuhn). If this happens very early in the pregnancy, this experience can be much like a menstrual period, and women may not know that they were pregnant. Miscarriages later in the pregnancy have to be treated as a birth, with labor induced. Losing a baby, even when the pregnancy is not advanced, is a very sad experience.

Unplanned pregnancies happen to both married and unmarried people. Sometimes the chosen method of birth control fails, but more often people fail to use protection or to use it carefully. While the news of an unexpected pregnancy comes to some like a tornado threatening to shake everything loose, to others it comes as a blessing. Everyone's circumstances are different.

Regardless of how unplanned pregnancies happen, they force some people to make difficult decisions.

- How will we provide for this baby's needs?
- Are we emotionally equipped to care for this baby?
- What adjustments will we need to make for this child to grow up healthy and strong?
- Can we do this?

> **How can people give up their baby for adoption?**

Giving a baby up for **adoption** requires a great deal of courage. Birthmothers, sometimes with the birthfather, make the decision in the best interest of the child and in difficult assessment of their own readiness and abilities to parent at the time. Enabling a childless couple to have a family and giving a child a better chance in life is a caring thing to do, but that doesn't make it easy. Some adoption arrangements allow birthparents to play an ongoing role in the child's life; others do not.

> **What is an abortion?**

> **Why would someone have an abortion?**

> **What happens when a person has an abortion?**

An **abortion** (uh-BORE-shun) ends a pregnancy and a life by choice. If done surgically, the lining of the uterus and the embryo or fetus are removed using a suction process, or drugs are given that cause the woman's body to discharge the embryo or fetus. An abortion can also be done medically: prescription medications taken by mouth can

130

make the uterus reject a newly conceived embryo, resulting in an abortion that resembles a woman's usual menstrual period.

Abortion is sometimes considered when pregnancy is threatening the life of the mother, when tests show that a fetus has no hope for survival; or when the pregnancy is the result of rape (forced sexual intercourse). Unfortunately many people also see abortion as a means of birth control, using it to end an inconvenient pregnancy. Abortion is not acceptable birth control.

Some people believe that abortion is wrong in every situation; others acknowledge "tragic conflicts of life with life." The decision to terminate a pregnancy brings an end to a life and must be made with prayer and very careful thought. Some who choose abortion feel deep regret later on. Those faced with this decision need loving support. They need to explore their feelings and to consider how this decision is going to affect them now and later on. Parents, pastors, physicians, friends, and the father of the unborn child are important persons to involve as the decision is made.

⚧ Sexting = Sex + Texting

"Sexting" or sex + texting is the name given to taking, sending, receiving, and forwarding semi-nude or naked photos from cell phones. Sometimes this is done to tease—trying to get a sexual reaction from a boyfriend or girlfriend. Sometimes sexting is seen as a harmless prank or joke—an attempt to embarrass someone for the amusement of others. Sometimes sexting is an attempt to get revenge. Regardless, someone is being abused in the process, and young persons may find themselves being arrested and charged as pornographers when these photos start circulating. Unauthorized or unwanted distribution of sexual photos could be considered sexual harassment. Once a photo has been taken and sent, the one who originally took or posed for the photo has no control over who will see it. The photo becomes a permanent part of Internet information. If a

> What is sexting? Is it bad? Why?

boyfriend or girlfriend started the whole thing, you might think it all very safe, but it's not.

You are old enough to consider the consequences of your actions, so consider this: Young people are finding their futures—college applications, scholarships, and jobs—permanently affected when "innocent" sexting spins out of control. Give thanks for the mind God gave you and avoid sexting!

STDs, HIV, and AIDS

What's an STD?

Can you get a disease from kissing?

Sexually transmitted diseases or STDs are infectious diseases that enter the body through sexual contact: primarily through intercourse or kissing. The viruses and bacteria travel in bodily fluids—blood, semen, vaginal fluids, and saliva, although rarely some can be transferred with skin-to-skin contact. When those fluids pass from an infected person to a sexual partner, the viruses or bacteria infect the partner.

A few STDs can be treated and cured. Some STD symptoms can be treated, but the disease remains in the body permanently where it can be passed to others. These are some of the symptoms:

- unusual odor or fluids discharged from the penis or vagina
- itching or burning genitals
- a rash or sore in or around the genitals, anus, or mouth
- abdominal pain or tenderness
- pain or burning during urination
- fatigue and/or night sweats

These symptoms do not automatically mean that a person has an STD, and a person can have an STD and have no symptoms at all. Or, these symptoms can indicate the presence of other diseases—those that are not sexually transmitted. However, persons who are sexually active and have any of these symptoms should to see their doctor. Be aware that certain STDs can spread from an infected expectant mother to her unborn child and can cause a variety of birth defects in the child.

Although having sexual relations with someone infected with HIV is the most common way for the virus to spread, it is not the only way. Sharing needles and syringes by users of illegal drugs is the second most common way. It is even possible to transmit the AIDS virus through the needles for tattooing, cosmetic body-piercing, and during blood transfusions. However, attention to sterilization of needles and procedures to test blood donations have nearly eliminated those risks.

HIV or AIDs is not spread through casual contact. An infected student at your school is not a threat. Using a toilet or a drinking fountain that has been used by someone with AIDS does not endanger you. Neither does playing sports or eating together.

Before getting married or before becoming sexually involved, persons who have been sexually active with others should be tested for STDs.

KNOW THIS: You cannot look at a person and tell if he or she has a sexually transmitted disease. Because AIDs symptoms may not appear until long after a person has been infected, it is usually not possible to tell whether or not a person has AIDs. The only way to be completely safe is the avoidance of all behavior that puts you at risk.

Who Is Most at Risk for STDs?

In the United States, of the approximately 19 million new infections that occur each year, almost half of them are diagnosed among people between the ages of 15 and 24.

What are all the diseases you can catch from sex and how?

There are more than 20 different STDs. Other than **acquired immunodeficiency syndrome** (uh-KWIRED ih-MUN-oh duh-FISH-un-see SIN-drohm) or **AIDS,** and **Human Immunodeficiency Virus** (ih-MYOO-noh-duh-FIH-shuhn-see) or **HIV,** the most common ones in the United States are **chlamydia** (kluh-MID-ee-uh), **gonorrhea** (gahn-uh-REE-uh), **syphilis** (SIF-ul-luhs), **genital herpes** (HER-peez), **genital human papillomavirus** (pa-pihl-LOH-muh-VIE-ruhs) or **HPV** (There is a vaccine recommended for girls to protect them from HPV-caused cervical cancer and genital warts. Many doctors recommend it.), **hepatitis B** (HEP-uh-TIE-tihs), **trichomoniasis** (TRIHK-uh-moh-NIE-uh-sihs), and **bacterial vaginosis** (VAJ-uh-NO-suhs). To thoroughly cover even these diseases would take much more space than what we have available, so you can research these diseases if you want more information. BUT KNOW THIS: once contracted, <u>these diseases will be with you for your lifetime</u>, some with painful periodic outbreaks. And, they can always be spread to your sexual partner.

Is sexual intercourse safe?

Abstinence from sexual intercourse is the only guaranteed way to avoid all of these diseases.

Is there any forgiveness?

What if you or someone you know has already made sexual mistakes? Can they be forgiven? Of course! Persons who recognize

their wrong-doing, ask for forgiveness, and change their behavior will be forgiven. Remember the woman who was brought to Jesus after being caught in adultery (having sexual intercourse with someone other than her husband)? The authorities were ready to stone her for her actions. With compassion Jesus pointed out that they too were sinners and had no right to judge the woman. He sent her on her way, not to return to her sins, but to live a faithful life.

When persons acknowledge their past, change their behavior, and trust in the goodness of God, God receives them and helps them begin a different kind of life.

Who's Going to Answer the Rest of My Questions?

We're guessing you still have a zillion questions. Each of your questions is important and deserves an answer. We hope you're finding answers to lots of those questions in this book, but you will no doubt have questions we didn't think of or didn't have space to answer.

Your parents can be a good source of answers. Although some may be too uncomfortable to answer, many parents want to talk with you about this all-important topic, but just don't know how to start the conversation. They may not know all the answers, but will search with you to find them and to help you understand the values of your family and church. Next, other family members like grandparents may be a good source.

If you are reading this book as part of the *Created by God* study, then you have or will have a Small Group Leader who experienced the study with you, and will continue to be available for your questions, and will keep those questions confidential. If you are not already part of a *Created by God* study, then we encourage you to attend. Group studies give everyone basic information, offer a chance to understand proper terms, allow everyone to ask his or her particular questions, and get people talking with one another. We have seen that many tweens are hesitant to attend such a study, but afterward are glad they did. Our experience shows that the church does the best job with human sexuality education. We know it's important to keep God in the answers! So, keep asking and you'll get the answers you need!

Now that you've read all this, take some deep breaths and then read the words of Philippians 4:8 out loud.

Stay close to persons who love you, who guide you, who forgive your fumbles, who celebrate your successes, and who know you as the wonderful, marvelous, glorious, fantastic creation of God that you are.

As you seek what is true, honorable, just, pure, pleasing, and commendable, you'll find your family, your friends, and your God will give you the strength you need to soar into a happy and faithful adulthood.

> **Finally, beloved, whatever is true, whatever is honorable,
> whatever is just, whatever is pure, whatever is pleasing,
> whatever is commendable, if there is any excellence
> and if there is anything worthy of praise,
> think about these things.**
>
> (Philippians 4:8)

Glossary

The numbers at the end of the definitions direct you to the pages where you will find more information about these terms.

abdomen (AB-doh-muhn). The belly. 26

abortion (uh-BORE-shun). Medically ending a pregnancy and a potential life by causing a woman's body to discharge the endometrium and the embryo or fetus before it is able to survive on its own, or surgically removing the endometrium and embryo or fetus. 130

abstinence (AB-stuh-nuhns). Living out the decision not to have sexual intercourse until one has committed his or her life to another person. The only 100 percent effective method for avoiding pregnancy and sexually transmitted diseases. 102

acne (ACK-nee). Pimples or blemishes that often appear on the face, chest, back, and elsewhere on the body caused by blocked oil glands. Can be particularly severe during adolescence and demands special care. 64

acquired immunodeficiency syndrome (uh-KWIRED ih-MUN-oh duh-FISH-un-see SIN-drohm) or **AIDS.** A disease caused by the Human Immunodeficiency Virus (HIV). AIDS causes the breakdown of the body's immune system, making it impossible for the body to fight off other diseases. AIDS is transmitted by the exchange of body fluids—primarily through sexual intercourse but also through the sharing of drug injection equipment with someone who has HIV and from infected mothers to their babies. 134

adolescence (a-doh-LES-sens). The period of physical, mental, emotional, and interpersonal growth between childhood and adulthood. A young person going through this period is referred to as an adolescent (a-doh-LES-sent). 15

adoption. Taking a child into a family by legal means and raising that child as one's own. 130

AIDS. See acquired immunodeficiency syndrome. 133, 134

amnion (AM-nee-uhn) or **amniotic sac** (am-nee-AH-tik). The thin membrane sac filled with a watery fluid called amniotic fluid that surrounds and protects the developing fetus in the uterus. 92

ampulla (am-POOL-uh). The widened or flared-out portion of the vas deferens near the prostate gland. 31, 32

anus (AY-nuhs). The opening where solid waste leaves the body. 26, 34

areola (air-ee-OH-lah). The darker circle of the breast that surrounds the nipple. 46, 48

bacterial vaginosis (VAJ-uh-NO-suhs). A sexually transmitted disease. 134

birth control. Preventing conception from taking place. 108

birth control pills. Artificial hormones a woman must take every day to prevent ovulation and therefore pregnancy. 108

bisexual (bie-SEKS-yoo-uhl). Having sexual feelings for both genders. 115

breasts. Two glands on the upper chest of both males and females, the growth of which is stimulated at puberty. In females, the breasts develop so that they can produce milk when the female gives birth to a baby. 26, 46, 48, 59

Breast Self-Examination (BSE). A monthly self-exam that all maturing girls and all women need to perform on their breasts, checking for changes or abnormalities. Males also need to periodically examine their breasts for changes and abnormalities. 49, 50, 51

breech. When a baby is in something other than a head-first position prior to birth. This position can complicate the delivery, sometimes making a surgical delivery necessary. 93

caesarean section (sih-ZARE-ee-uhn). See surgical delivery. 93

cervical cap (SER-vih-cuhl). Similar to a diaphragm but smaller and fits securely to seal off the cervix. See diaphragm. 109

cervix (SER-viks). The lower, narrow portion of the uterus that extends into the vagina. The cervix must open or widen (dilate) in order to allow the baby to move into the vagina during birth. 35, 36

chlamydia (kluh-MID-ee-uh). A sexually transmitted disease. 134

chromosomes (KROH-muh-sohmz). Tiny rods in the center of every cell of every living thing that carry the inherited characteristics from parents. Human reproductive cells (ova and sperm) contain 23 individual chromosomes while all other cells have 46 (23 pairs). 43

cilia (SILL-ee-uh). Tiny hairs such as those lining the fallopian tubes in females and the vas deferens in males. These cilia move the ova through fallopian tubes and the sperm through the vas deferens. 36, 52

circumcision (sir-cum-SIZH-un). The surgical removal of the foreskin—the loose layer of skin that extends over the glans or head of the penis when a boy is born. One who receives this operation has been circumcised (SIR-cum-sized). 28, 29

clitoris (KLIT-uh-ris). The small, cylinder-shaped, highly sensitive female organ located at the top of the inner labia. 33, 34

conception (kuhn-SEP-shun). When the chromosomes and genes from the ovum and the sperm have united to form a combination unlike any other that has ever been or will ever be, you have a whole new idea or concept for a human being. 83, 88

condom (KON-duhm). A thin sheath, usually of rubber or latex that looks like a long, rolled-up, oversized balloon. It is carefully placed on the erect penis before sexual intercourse and carefully removed after ejaculation to prevent the spread of disease and/or to prevent pregnancy. 109

conjoined twins. Identical twins are formed by the partial division of the blastocyst into two clusters. Where the division is incomplete, one or more parts of the body are shared by both babies. Also called Siamese twins. 97

contraception (KON-truh-SEHP-shuhn). Any means for preventing pregnancy. 110

contract (kuhn-TRACT). See contractions. 92

contractions (kuhn-TRACK-shuns). The sudden shortening of the muscles in the uterus that helps to push the baby into the vagina and out of the mother's body. 92

cremaster muscle (krih-MASS-ter). A small muscle from which the testicles are suspended in the scrotum. 31

date rape. When a female is forced against her will to have sex with someone she is dating. 106

delivery. The mother and medical team working together to get the baby safely out of the mother's body. 92

diaphragm (DIE-uh-fram). A soft rubber dome or cap that is filled with a spermicide and inserted into the vagina before sexual intercourse to prevent pregnancy by blocking and immobilizing sperm. 109

dilate (DIE-late) or **dilation.** The opening or widening and softening of the cervix, allowing for the vaginal delivery of a baby. 92

ejaculation (e-JACK-yoo-LAY-shun). The release or squirting of semen from the penis caused by the squeezing of muscles and the prostate gland during orgasm. 31, 61

embryo (EM-bree-oh). An unborn human from about the eighth day after conception until the third month of pregnancy. 90

endocrine glands (EHN-doh-krihn). These are glands that secrete or send the fluids they produce directly into the bloodstream. Two examples are the ovaries and testicles. 43

endometrium (ehn-doh-MEE-tree-uhm). The inner wall or lining of the uterus. 36, 52

epididymis (ep-uh-DID-uh-mis). A mass of tiny tubes attached to the back of each testicle; the sperm cells mature as they move through the tubes. 31, 32

erect (ih-REKT) or **erection.** When sexual stimulation causes blood to rush to the genital area, filling the sponge-like tissue inside the shaft and resulting in the enlargement and hardening of the penis or the clitoris. 58, 60

estrogen (ESS-truh-juhn). The hormone that causes female sexual growth and development. 44

fallopian tubes (fuh-LOH-pee-unh). The two tubes that branch out from either side of the upper part of the uterus, through which the ova pass from the ovaries to the uterus. 35, 36

feminine (FEHM-uh-nin). Qualities associated with being female. Femininity (fehm-uh-NIN-uh-tee) is how a person expresses her understanding of what it means to be female. 78, 79

fertilization (FER-tuhl-uh-ZAY-shun). When the sperm successfully burrows into the ovum, releases its tail, and the outer layer of the ovum seals itself to prevent other sperm from getting in. 90

fetus (fee-TUHS). An unborn human from about the third month of pregnancy until birth. 90, 91

flaccid (FLA-sid). When the penis is soft, limp, or not erect. 59

follicle (FALL-uh-kuhl). Tiny sacs or capsules in the ovaries that each contain an ovum. 36

foreplay (FOR-play). Sex play where a couple enjoys physical closeness that precedes and prepares their bodies to have sexual intercourse. 86

foreskin (FOR-skin). The loose layer of skin that covers the glans or tip of a male's penis at birth and is sometimes removed with a surgical procedure called circumcision. 29, 32

fraternal. A multiple birth that began with the release of more than one ovum and the fertilization of those ova by different sperm. 96

gay. A homosexual person. 115

gender (JEN-der). Being male or female, having male or female reproductive systems. 43

genes (jeenz). The part of every body cell, located on the chromosomes, that carries information about characteristics that one inherits from either or both parents. 43

genital herpes (HER-peez). A sexually transmitted disease. 134

genital human papillomavirus (pa-pihl-LOH-muh-VIE-ruhs) or **HPV.** A sexually transmitted disease. 134

genitals (JEN-uh-tuhls) or **genitalia** (JEN-uh-TAIL-yuh). The external sex organs (the ones we can see) that identify us as male or female. 26, 27

glans (glanz). The head or tip of the penis or the clitoris. 28, 29

gonorrhea (gahn-uh-REE-uh). A sexually transmitted disease. 134

hepatitis B (HEP-uh-TIE-tihs). A sexually transmitted disease. 134

heredity (huh-REHD-uh-tee). Characteristics passed from parents to offspring. 43

heterosexual (HEHT-uh-roh-SEHK-shoo-uhl). Having sexual feelings for the other gender. 115

HIV. See Human Immunodeficiency Virus. 133, 134

homosexual (HOH-moh-SEHK-shoo-uhl). Having sexual feelings for one's own gender. 115

hormones (HOR-mohns). Chemical substances produced by glands that serve as a communication system. These chemicals are "messages" traveling through the bloodstream that enable the glands to regulate the functioning of other organs. 30, 43

HPV. See genital human papillomavirus. 134

Human Immunodeficiency Virus (ih-MYOO-noh-duh-FIH-shuhn-see) or **HIV**. A virus that attacks the body's immune system—the system that fights off disease. Without proper medical treatment can cause AIDS. 133, 134

hymen (HI-muhn). A layer of stretchy tissue about the thickness of plastic wrap located around the opening to the vagina. It may be worn away by general physical activity—probably more quickly as a result of vigorous athletic activity or stretching movement. It also can be torn during first sexual intercourse and result in a small amount of bleeding. Hymens look very different from one female to the next, and some women are born without a hymen. 33, 34

identical. A multiple birth that began with the complete division of a single fertilized ovum, forming two or more babies that are completely alike. 96

incest (IN-sest). Sexual intercourse between close relatives; a practice forbidden in most cultures and illegal in most countries. 105

intercourse. See sexual intercourse. 87

intimacy (IN-tuh-muh-see). A close relationship, a growing and deepening friendship between people based on things like openness, respect, trust, selflessness, and compassion. Intimacy is something that can happen between any two people who are willing to work at it. 72

intrauterine device (in-tra-YOO-tuhr-in) or **IUD**. A birth control device that interferes with the movement of sperm. It must be inserted into the uterus by a doctor to prevent pregnancy and removed by a doctor when a couple wants to get pregnant. 108

labia (LAY-bee-uh). Two sets of folds of skin that are part of the vulva. The outer or major labia surround the openings to the vagina and urethra. The inner or minor labia are inside and sometimes hidden by the outer labia, although in some females the inner labia are larger and cover the outer labia. In Latin the word labia means "lips." 33, 34

labor. The stage of giving birth during which the cervix dilates or opens up, allowing the contractions of the uterine muscles to work with the mother's bearing down to push the baby from the uterus into the vagina in preparation for delivery. 92

lesbian (LEZ-bee-uhn). A female homosexual. 115

lobes. Sections inside a woman's breast where milk is produced. 46, 48

masculine (MASS-kyuh-lin). Qualities associated with being male. Masculinity (MASS-kyuh-LIN-uh-tee) is how a person expresses his understanding of what it means to be male. 78, 79

masturbation (MASS-ter-BAY-shun). The deliberate touching, rubbing, or stroking of one's genitals to create his or her own sexual pleasure. 52, 122

menopause (MEHN-uh-pahz). The time in a woman's life—usually between the ages of 45 and 55—during which ovulation and menstruation slows down and then ceases, making pregnancy no longer possible. 54

menstrual cycle (MEHN-stroo-uhl). See menstruation. 52, 53

menstrual period (MEHN-stroo-uhl). The series of four to seven days when the lining of the uterus breaks down and is discharged from the body. Menstrual means "monthly" and period refers to a specific span of time, so this is a span of time that happens monthly. 53

menstruation (mehn-STRAY-shun). The discharge of blood, secretions, and tissue from the uterus that females experience for four to seven days, about once a month. The entire process is called the menstrual (MEHN-stroo-uhl) cycle. The time during which the discharge takes place is called the menstrual period or simply the period. 52, 53

milk ducts (duhkts). Channels inside the breast through which the mother's milk flows to the nipple during breast-feeding. 46, 48

miscarriage (MISS-kair-ihj). See spontaneous abortion. 129

molestation (MAH-lehs-TAY-shun). The sexual abuse of a child. 104

morning sickness. The upset stomach that some pregnant women experience, particularly during the first three months of pregnancy, as their bodies adjust to the new life growing inside of them. It is so named because it often takes place in the morning. 128

Natural Family Planning. In order to avoid pregnancy, a couple watches carefully for signs of ovulation—such as the woman's body temperature—and avoids sexual intercourse on days when conception is possible. 108

navel (NAY-vuhl). The scar left on the abdomen after the stump of the umbilical cord that remains has dried up and fallen off. 93

nipple. The tip or center of the outside of the breast. 46, 48

nocturnal emission (nock-TER-nul ee-MISH-uhn). The ejaculation of built-up semen that occurs during sleep and is often associated with sexual dreams. Also called a wet dream. 62

oral sex. One person using his or her mouth to stimulate the genitals of another person. 123

orgasm (OR-gaz-uhm). The pleasant tensing and pulsing of muscles in the genital area that spreads to the rest of the body and signals the most intense point of excitement in sexual activity. 61

ova (OH-vah). Female reproductive cells and the plural of ovum. 36, 52

ovaries (OH-vuh-reez). Two almond-sized female reproductive glands in which ova develop and sex hormones are produced. (Ovary is a single gland.) 35, 36

ovulation (ah-vyuh-LAY-shun). The maturing or ripening and release of an ovum from an ovary, occurring about once a month. 52

ovum (OH-vuhm). A female reproductive cell. 36, 52, 89

penis (PEE-nuhs). The cylinder-shaped part of the male genitals through which urine and semen pass, made up of the shaft, glans, and foreskin. 28, 29, 32

period. See menstrual period. 53

pituitary gland (pih-TOO-uh-tare-ee). An endocrine gland positioned in the center of the brain, directly behind the eyes. Secretes hormones that control body processes. 43

placenta (pluh-SEN-tuh). A spongy organ containing a network of blood vessels that is attached to the endometrium during pregnancy; it enables nourishment and oxygen to get from mother to baby, and for carbon dioxide and waste products to be processed. 90

pleasuring. Sex play where a couple enjoys physical closeness. See foreplay. 86

pornography (pore-NAHG-ruh-fee). Sexually explicit photos, art, movies, or books containing naked images of people and images of people engaged in sexual acts, treating them as objects rather than as persons; images promoting sexual relations between children and between adults and children; images linking sex with violence. 126

pregnancy (PREG-nun-see). The period from conception to birth. The condition of having a developing embryo or fetus within the female body. 36

premenstrual syndrome (pree-MEN-stroo-uhl SIHN-drohm) or **PMS.** The effects that hormones have on the female body before her period; may include mood swings, irritability, sadness or depression, swelling or bloating (retaining fluid). 54

prenatal (pree-NAY-tuhl) **care.** Medical care for mothers and babies during pregnancy.

prostate gland (PROSS-tate). A ring-shaped organ surrounding the male urethra that adds fluid to the semen and squeezes to help force the mixture of semen and sperm into the urethra during ejaculation. 31, 32

prostitute (PROSS-tuh-toot). A person who is paid to perform sexual acts. 107

puberty (PEW-bur-tee). The period when the body changes from that of a child to that of an adult; the sex organs mature and begin to produce mature ova or sperm. 25

pubic hair (PEW-bick). Hair that appears in the genital area during puberty, becoming coarser and curlier and increasing in amount as puberty progresses. 26, 27, 46

rape. Forced sexual intercourse. 106

rectum (RECK-tum). The lower end of the large intestine, ending at the anus. 35

reproduction (REE-pro-DUC-shun). The process by which all living things create more of their own kind.

sanitary pad. A pad of absorbent cotton with adhesive strips worn inside the underpants to absorb the menstrual discharge. Also called a sanitary napkin. 53

scrotum (SKRO-tum). The pouch of skin beneath the penis that contains the testicles. 28, 30

semen (SEE-muhn). The whitish fluid, about the consistency of egg whites, that is produced in the seminal vesicles; mobilizes the sperm and carries them out of the penis during ejaculation. Also called seminal fluid. 31

seminal vesicles (SEM-uh-nuhl VESS-ih-kuhls). Two small pouches located at the back of the male prostate gland, where semen (seminal fluid) is produced. 31, 32

sex. Being female or male. Comes from the Latin word sexus which means "to divide." The human race is divided into two basic groups or genders—female and male—according to their functions or responsibilities related to reproduction.

sexting. Taking, sending, receiving, and forwarding naked photos from cell phones. 131

sexual. Having a gender and either a male or female role in reproduction.

sexual abuse. When one person uses sexual actions or sexual language to hurt, frighten, embarrass, or take advantage of another person. 104

sexual intercourse. Sexual activity where the penis is inserted into the vagina. 86, 87

sexuality. The sum of a person's gender, sexual orientation, behaviors, and attitude toward himself or herself and others as it is shaped by being either male or female.

sexually transmitted diseases or **STDs**. A variety of diseases caused by bacteria or viruses that spread from one person to another through sexual activity. 132

sexual orientation (or-ee-en-TAY-shun). Whether one is sexually attracted to or sexually active with one's own sex, the other sex, or persons of both sexes. 115

shaft. The cylinder-shaped portion of the penis or of the clitoris. 28, 29

sonogram (SAHN-uh-gram) or ultrasound. A picture of a fetus inside the uterus made by bouncing sound waves off of the baby.

sperm. Reproductive cell or cells produced in the testicles. 30, 89

spermicide (SPER-mih-side). A sperm-killing foam, cream, or jelly inserted deep in the vagina prior to sexual intercourse. 109

spontaneous abortion (spahn-TAY-nee-uhs ah-BORE-shuhn). When the mother's body expels an embryo or fetus from the uterus before it is mature enough to survive, usually due either to some abnormality that would have prevented the baby from developing normally, or a problem with the mother's ability to support the full pregnancy. Sometimes called a miscarriage. 129

stereotype (STAIR-ee-uh-type). A very narrowly defined image of what everyone within a group ought to be like. People who operate out of stereotypes believe that if you know one thing (like gender) about a person, you know everything about that person. Stereotypes do not recognize the individuality of each person. 78

surgical delivery. When a baby is removed from the mother's body through an incision into the abdomen and uterus; also called a Caesarean section or C-section. 93

syphilis (SIF-uh-luhs). A sexually transmitted disease. 134

tampon (TAM-pahn). A roll of absorbent material that is inserted into the vagina to absorb the menstrual discharge. 53

testicles (TESS-tih-kuhls). The egg-shaped male reproductive glands, suspended in the scrotum, that produce sperm and sex hormones. 30, 32

testicular self-examination (tess-TIC-yuh-luhr) or **TSE**. A monthly self-exam that all maturing boys and all men need to do to check for changes or abnormalities in the testicles. 57, 58

testosterone (tess-TOSS-tuh-rone). The hormone that causes male sexual growth and development. 55

trichomoniasis (TRIHK-uh-moh-NIE-uh-sihs). A sexually transmitted disease. 134

tubal ligation (TOO-buhl lie-GAY-shun). A surgical procedure for sterilization in females. The fallopian tubes are cut, tied, sealed, or otherwise blocked off, either through an incision in the abdomen or through the vagina. Ova, unable to travel through the tubes, are absorbed by the body. 110

umbilical cord (umh-BILL-uh-kuhl). The cord connecting the unborn infant to the placenta through which the fetus receives oxygen and nourishment and gets rid of waste materials. 90, 100

urethra (yoo-REE-thruh). The narrow tube through which urine passes out of the body from the bladder. In females the urethra is totally separate from the vagina. In males the urethra is also a part of the reproductive system, serving as a passageway for semen. 26, 27, 32, 33, 35

uterus (YOO-ter-us). The muscular, hollow organ in females, shaped like a light bulb or upside-down pear, in which babies grow and are nourished before birth. Also called the womb. 35, 36

vagina (vuh-JIE-nuh). An elastic, muscular passage leading from the uterus to the outside of the body. Receives the erect penis during sexual intercourse and allows a baby to pass from the womb and out of the mother's body during delivery. 33, 35, 36

vas deferens (VAZ DEHF-uhr-unhz). The tube connected to the epididymis through which sperm travel and are stored. Also called the spermatic duct, sperm duct, or simply the vas. 31, 32

vasectomy (vah-SEHK-tuh-me). The surgical procedure for sterilization in males. On both sides of the scrotum, a small incision is made, and the vas deferens is cut, tied, sealed, or otherwise blocked off. Normal ejaculation of semen continues, but the semen no longer contains sperm. Sperm continue to be produced, but they are reabsorbed by the body. 110

virgin (VUHR-gin). Originally referred to a young woman who had never experienced sexual intercourse. Today it refers to any female or male who has not experienced sexual intercourse. 33

vulnerability (VUHL-ner-uh-BILL-uh-tee). Able to be hurt or the need for relationships with other people. Vulnerability means that there are some things we cannot do on our own. When entering into relationships there is also the possibility that we could be hurt, and that makes us vulnerable. 73

vulva (VUL-vuh). The genitals or external sex organs of the female. Includes the labia, clitoris, and the openings to the vagina and urethra. 33

womb. (WOOM). See uterus. 35, 36